Floral Dimensions Quilt

Create your own three-dimensional appliqué quilt

Pauline Ineson

Contents

Introduction

More than sixty of my students have made the award winning Floral Dimensions Quilt. This book describes how to stitch, quilt and make one of your very own. It also includes how to join the squares using my Back-to-Front technique which is mostly machine sewn. The templates needed are supplied full size within each chapter. You will also need my *Floral Dimensions* book, published by David & Charles, for instructions on how to create the three-dimensional flowers. This can be purchased from good book stores and via my website: www.paulineineson.co.uk.

Begonia Square

This section describes the making and quilting of the Begonia Square.
Refer to the *Floral Dimensions* book for instructions on making the
begonia and marigold flowers.

Requirements
- Fabric: for stems, centre leaves, teardrops at the corners and sides,
  circles, centre flower, begonias and begonia centres
- Machine sewing thread: cotton or polyester to match your fabrics
- Tear-away stabiliser: small piece
- Fusible interfacing: small strip
- Steam-A-Seam fusible web: 12in (30.5cm) square approximately
- Fray Check seam sealant
- Heatproof template plastic or Mylar 'Perfect Circles'
- Fabric glue stick and Clover Fabric Folding Pen (optional)
- Background fabric: 14in (35.5cm) square
- Wadding (batting): 14in (35.5cm) square plus small amount for stems,
  leaves and petals
- Backing and sashing fabric

Start by tracing the design onto the right side of the background fabric.

Begonia Stems

1 Trace the four stem shapes onto Steam-A-Seam and cut them out on the line.

2 Remove the backing paper and iron the stem shapes on to the wrong side of the fabric, leaving about 1in (2.5cm) between them to allow for turnings. Cut the fabric about ¼in (6mm) from the edge of the fusible web and then turn the fabric over the edge of the Steam-A-Seam using your favourite method as described in the **Floral Dimensions** book.

3 Carefully remove the second backing paper from the Steam-A-Seam, keeping the edges turned, and place the stems onto a piece of wadding, wrong sides down. Tack (baste) in place.

4 Trim the wadding just underneath the edges of the stems so that it doesn't show on the right side. Sew the stems to the background using a blind hem or buttonhole appliqué stitch.

Centre Leaves

1 Trace four centre leaves and four reverse centre leaves onto Steam-A-Seam and then cut them out on the line.

2 Peel off the backing paper and iron the leaves on to the wrong side of the fabric, leaving about 1in (2.5cm) between each leaf for turnings. Trim the fabric about ¼in (6mm) from the edge of the fusible web. Turn the edges over the fusible web as before.

3 Carefully remove the second backing paper and then press the edges again. Place the leaves onto a piece of wadding, wrong sides down and tack (baste) in place.

4 Trim the wadding just underneath the edges of the leaves so that it doesn't show on the right side. Sew the leaves to the background using a blind hem or buttonhole appliqué stitch.

Teardrops and Teardrop Petals

1 Trace eight teardrops, four teardrop petals and four reverse teardrop petals onto Steam-A-Seam. Cut each shape on the line.

2 Peel the backing paper off the shapes and iron them on to the wrong side of your chosen fabric, leaving about 1in (2.5cm) between each shape for turnings. Cut each shape out about ¼in (6mm) from the edges of the fusible web. Turn the edges over the Steam-A-Seam as before.

3 Remove the second backing paper from each shape and press the edges down again. Place each shape, wrong side down onto a piece of wadding and tack (baste) in place.

4 Trim the wadding just under the edges of the shapes so that it doesn't show on the right side. Sew the teardrops and teardrop petals to the background using a blind hem or buttonhole appliqué stitch.

Circles

Make four ⅝in (1.6cm) diameter circles and four ½in (1.3cm) diameter circles. You will need a template the same size as your finished circle that is reasonably heatproof. There will be a layer of fabric between the iron and the template so it won't be touching the iron. The best templates to use are pre-cut circles called 'Perfect Circles' made from Mylar template plastic, which is heatproof. They come in a set with four each of sixteen different sizes ranging from $5/16$in (8mm) to 2in (5cm). If you do not have a set of these, then you can make your own circle templates from Mylar template plastic or thin card. Use a coin or the end of a reel of thread as a circle guide. Draw around the template on the wrong side of your fabric.

There are two methods you can use to prepare the circles, method A or B, as follows.
Method A: Sew a gathering stitch (length 3.0) approximately ⅛in (3mm) from the edge of the circle. Use an open-toe foot, don't fix the beginning and end and leave thread tails (see Fig 1). Keeping the thread tails away from the scissors, trim each circle about ⅛in from the stitching line (Fig 2). If you want to add a little padding under the circles, then cut out circles of wadding slightly smaller than your finished circles. Place the wadding circle, if used, in the centre of the wrong side of the fabric circle and your template on top. Knot the thread tails that are on the wrong side and pull up the threads on the right side tightly (Fig 3). Spray starch, remove the template and press again.

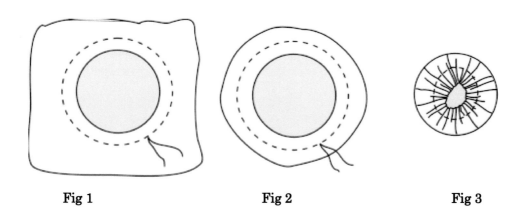

| Fig 1 | Fig 2 | Fig 3 |

Method B: For this method, cut your fabric approximately ⅛in–¼in (3mm–6mm) from the drawn line and then place the heatproof template in the centre on the wrong side. Apply a Clover Fabric Folding Pen to the fabric edge and then a Sewline Glue Stick. Using the side edge of a mini iron or small iron, press the fabric edge over the top of the template. When all the edges have been turned, remove the template plastic and press again. Place a slightly smaller circle of wadding beneath the circle if desired before appliquéing to the background.

Begonias
Follow the instructions in the **Floral Dimensions** book to make eight begonia flowers. Hand sew the flowers to the background by catching the underneath of each large petal.

Marigold
Refer to the **Floral Dimensions** book to make the marigold, that is, the ruched and coiled flower in the centre.

Finishing the Square

1 Pin the appliquéd square to the wadding and backing to make your quilting sandwich. If you are going to use my 'back-to-front' method to join the squares together you will need to follow the instructions for making up in the Back-to-Front Joining Technique section (Layering the Appliquéd Squares before Quilting), to ensure that the backing is marked correctly at this point.

2 I have used three different quilting patterns on the squares – crosshatching, parallel lines and echo quilting. I crosshatched this square, which is marked as follows. Using an easily removable marker, draw a line 1in (2.5cm) in from each edge, resulting in a 12in (30.5cm) square. If you are using my back-to-front technique then these will be the tacking (basting) lines. Mark every 1in (2.5cm) along each of these lines, beginning and ending at a corner. Join the marks with diagonal lines. Skip over areas that have appliqué shapes – you won't be quilting across these.

3 Pin or tack (baste) the layers together securely.

4 Choose the threads to quilt the squares. Cotton or rayon would be best, although a polyester one could be used. The colour should match closely with the fabric. I used the same 40 weight rayon in the top and the bobbin. A different shade could be used in the bobbin but check the tension carefully to make sure you don't see any of the bottom thread on the top or the top thread on the bottom.

5 Use a quilting machine needle if you have one and a walking foot. Make sure you start with thread tails and adjust your machine to a stitch length 3.0. If your top and bottom threads match then you can 'fix' or secure the stitches at the beginning but leave thread tails. This means lots of ends to pull through and bury but gives a much better result than cutting them off. If the two threads are different shades, using the fix may result in blobs of the top colour showing on the back. If you choose not to use the fix function, you will have to pull the threads through to the back, knot them and bury the ends. Use an easy-threading needle to save time.

6 When you reach an appliqué shape where the quilting line continues on the other side, fix the stitch (if using), lift the presser foot and pull out the top and bottom thread about 4in (10.2cm) to the side of the machine with your index finger. When these threads are cut in half, this will leave them long enough to pull through and bury. Move the fabric and position the needle on the other side of the appliqué shape at the beginning of the next line and continue as before.

7 Bury the thread tails after sewing a few lines. If you leave them all to the end they are likely to get sewn in and be really difficult to separate.

8 This step is optional. Quilt around the outside of all of the flowers and leaves – quilting in the ditch of these motifs will create an attractive outline of them on the back of the quilt. You may need to use a narrow presser foot or zipper foot in some areas rather than the walking foot.

9 Hand sew the marigold flower to the centre of the square to finish.

Begonia Square Templates

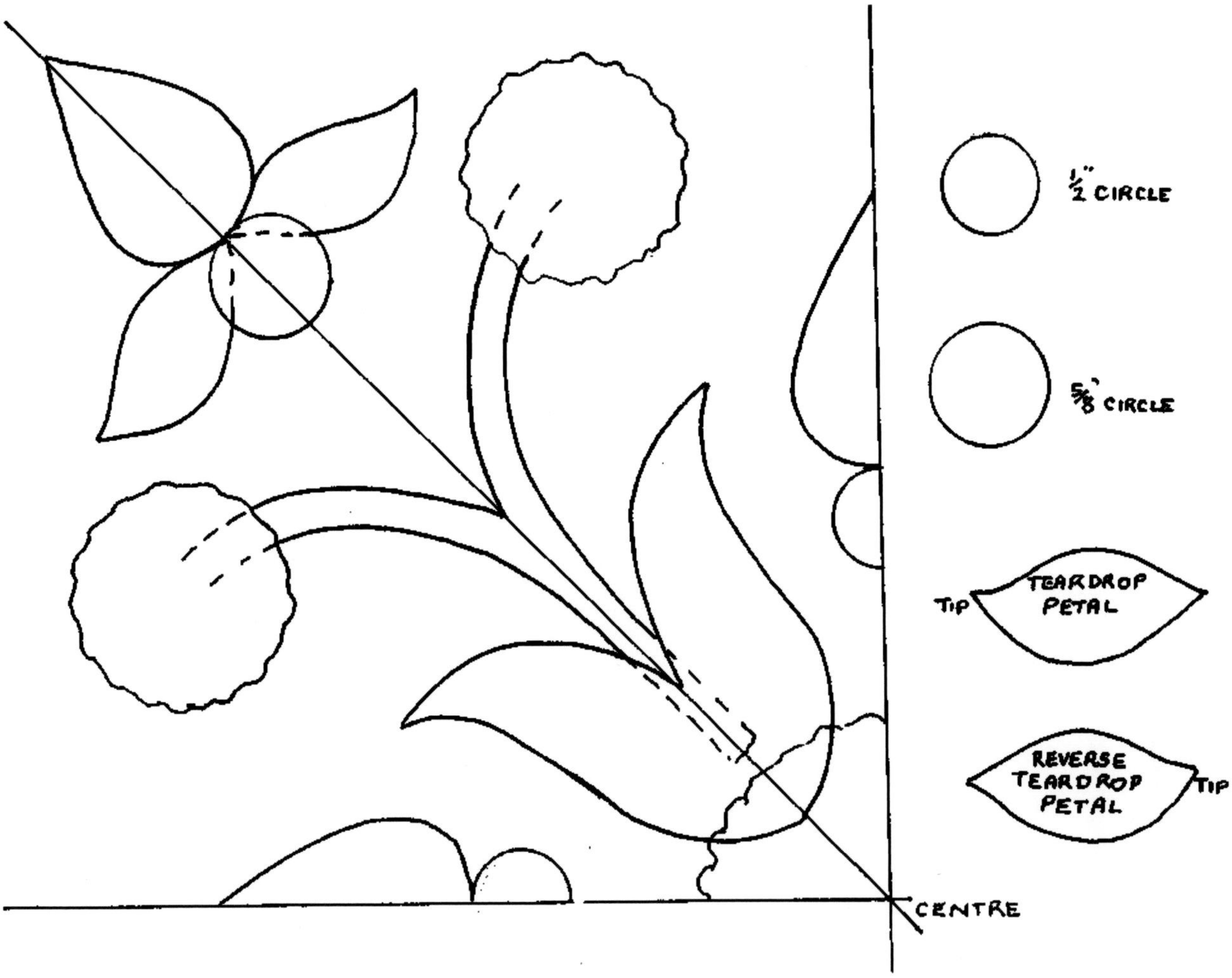

$\frac{1}{2}$" CIRCLE

$\frac{5}{8}$" CIRCLE

TIP — TEARDROP PETAL

REVERSE TEARDROP PETAL — TIP

CENTRE

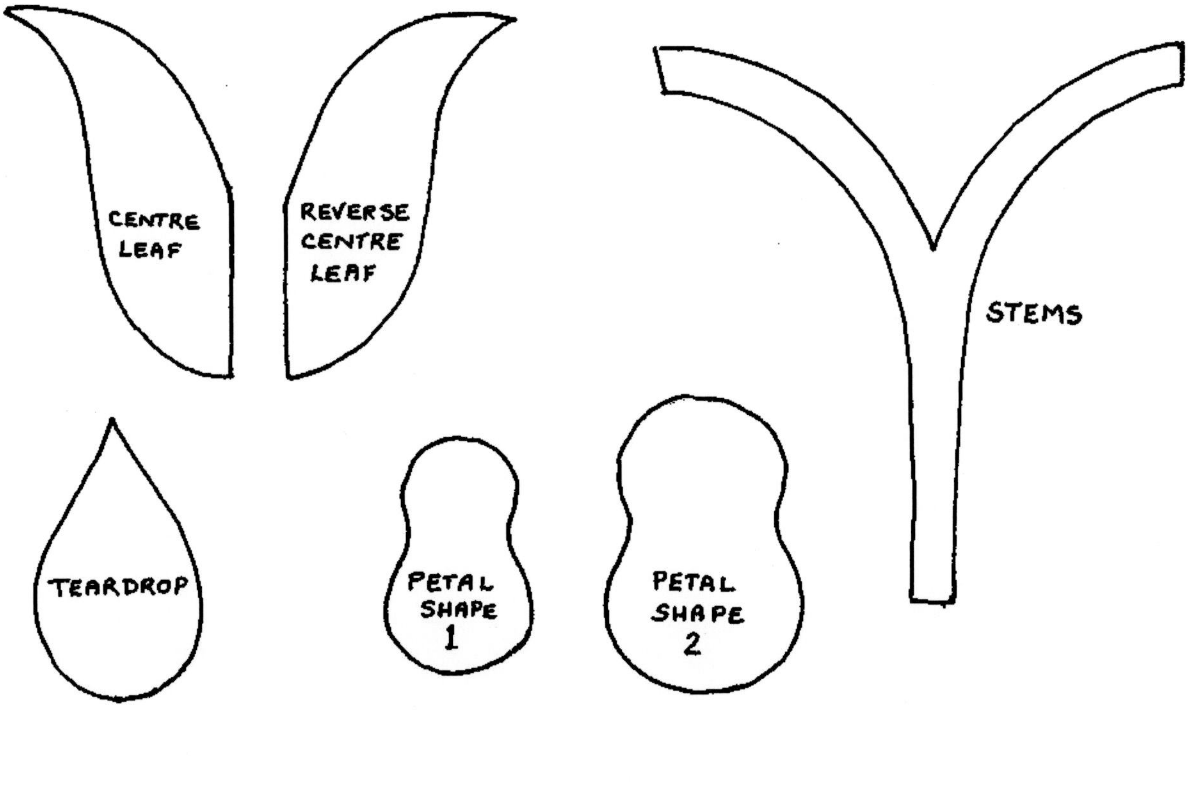

CENTRE LEAF

REVERSE CENTRE LEAF

STEMS

TEARDROP

PETAL SHAPE 1

PETAL SHAPE 2

Celtic Square

This section describes the making and quilting of the Celtic Square,
in particular showing how the bias strips are created and the
appliqué is worked.

Requirements
- Fabric: 19in (48.2cm) square or a fat quarter for bias strips, and about 6in
  (15.2cm) square of two different contrasting fabrics for the insets
- Machine sewing thread: cotton or polyester to match your fabrics
- Steam-A-Seam fusible web: two 6in (15.2cm) squares
- Fusible web for bias strips: $^{3}/_{16}$in (5mm) wide x 200in (508cm) long approximately
- Bias tape maker ¼in (6mm) or bias bar ¼in (6mm)
- Background fabric: 14in (35.5cm) square
- Wadding: 14in (35.5cm) square
- Backing and sashing fabric
- Light box (optional)

Making the Bias Tape

There are two different methods for making fusible bias tape, Method A or B, as follows.

Method A: Make the tape as you do for bias stems (refer to the **Floral Dimensions** book). You will need to cut your bias strips 1in (2.5cm) wide – twice as wide as the finished tape plus ½in (1.3cm) seam allowance (¼in/6mm on either edge) – and then iron the fusible web to the back after you have made it.

Method B: In this method the strips are cut fractionally wider than ½in (1.3cm) – twice as wide as the finished tape – and the web is ironed to the back of the tape as it is being made. Without any seam allowance, this gives a flatter more precise tape and is therefore more suited for Celtic designs, whereas a slightly raised, less accurate tape made with a bias bar would be better suited for stems. The following instructions are for the tape maker method, as the bias bar method has been explained in the **Floral Dimensions** book. You will need a bias tape maker the same size as the finished width of your tape with the facility to feed a fusible web through. You can use one without this facility and simply iron the web to the back of the tape when it is made. I used a 6mm (¼in) bias tape maker and $^3/_{16}$in (5mm) fusible web for the Celtic design.

1 Starch your fabric and then cut ½in (1.3cm) wide bias strips to total approximately 200in (508cm). Starched fabric is easier to work with.

2 Feed the end of the tape through the tape maker with the wrong side up. Use a pin to help move the end through. Feed the web through the slot at the top of the bias maker with the backing paper on top.

3 Pin the end of the tape to the right-hand side of an ironing board or mat if you are right-handed, or to the left side if you are left-handed.

4 Hold the iron with one hand and slowly move the tape maker back along the bias strip with the other hand, pressing the turned tape as you go, right next to the tape maker. I found that a mini iron is best for this. When you have about 1in (2.5cm) of finished tape, feed the web over the top so that the iron is over both the tape and the web. Continue ironing the two together, making sure that you don't stretch the bias strip by pulling the maker too tightly. This will make the strip narrower, minimising the edges that are turned. Continually check that the bias strip is always centred under the maker – don't let it veer off to one side. The narrower the finished tape, the more difficult it is because the edges that are turned are so narrow. If an edge pops out, just cut the tape off and start another length. Short lengths can be joined where they go under another strip in the design. If you find it difficult to apply the web at the same time, make the tape first and then iron the web to the back afterwards.

Adding the Insets

1 Using an easily removable marking pen on the right side of the background fabric, draw a line across the centre from one side to the other, and then another one across the centre from top to bottom. Trace the pattern four times, lining the centre point under the centre cross of the lines you have drawn and keeping the design centred.

2 Draw around Inset Shape 3 and Inset Shape 4 four times on Steam-A-Seam fusible web, on the side that has the web attached, and then rough cut them out.

3 Peel off the backing paper from the Steam-A-Seam, leaving the web on the paper that has the drawings. Place the web side of the paper to the wrong side of the inset fabric and press in place. Cut out the shapes on the line.

4 If you want to 'fussy cut' your inset fabric, omit steps 2 and 3 and draw the inset shape on template plastic and cut it out. Choose the area on your fabric that works best. Place the template over the top on the right side of the fabric and trace the flower or design that is on the fabric onto the template plastic. Draw around the edge of the template plastic on the fabric. Use the template to mark the other insets by placing it over the same flower or design each time and drawing around the edge. Next cut a piece of fusible web large enough to cover the first shape you drew around, peel off the backing paper and stick the piece that still has the web attached underneath the drawn shape onto the wrong side of the fabric. Iron in place and then cut out the shape on the line. Repeat for the remaining shapes.

5 Peel off the second backing paper. Place the shapes, right side up, in the windows of the design on the background fabric. Make sure they cover the lines evenly so that the bias tape will cover all the raw edges. Press in place.

6 Repeat for the remaining inset shapes with the second fabric. You will need eight of Inset Shape 1 and four of Inset Shape 2.

Applying the Bias Tape
1 Press the tape to the background, peeling off the backing paper from the fusible web as you go and mitring the points as follows. Draw a bisecting line through each angle where the tape will be mitred – these need to be about 5cm (2in) long towards the inside of the shape (Fig 1).

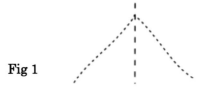

Fig 1

2 Place the background fabric on a lace-shaping board or ironing board. When you reach a bisecting line, place a pin at the outer point of the mitre and another at the inner point of the mitre along the bisecting line (Fig 2). The pins should go through the tape, the fabric and the board at an angle that is as flat as possible to the board, pointing away from the edge of the tape.

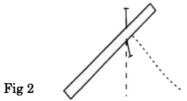

Fig 2

3 Fold the tape back on top of itself. Remove the pin at the inner point and replace through both layers of tape and into the board (Fig 3). You should have a small pleat of tape at the inner point.

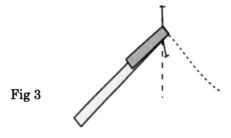

Fig 3

12

4 Now flip the tape over and continue placing the tape over the pattern line (Fig 4 and Fig 5). Make sure the pattern line is always in the centre of the tape underneath and any joins are beneath where two or more tapes cross.

Fig 4   Fig 5

5 The design is in two continuous parts. Begin with the design marked in a broken line on the pattern and then the design marked in a solid line. Place tear-away stabiliser underneath. Machine both edges of the tape using the blind hem or buttonhole appliqué stitch. Stop where the tape goes underneath and start again where it comes out from the other side. Sew the design marked with a broken line before ironing the tape on the design marked in a solid line. Carefully remove the tear-away stabiliser.

Finishing the Square

Pin the appliquéd square to the wadding and backing to make your quilting sandwich. If you are going to use my 'back-to-front' method to join the squares together you will need to follow the instructions for making up in the Back-to-Front Joining Technique section (Layering the Appliquéd Squares before Quilting), to ensure that the backing is marked correctly at this point. I chose to echo quilt my square, as described below. Echo quilting is the term used for stitching that echoes the shape of an appliquéd or quilted design, similar to ripples on a pond (see the pictures below). The lines are anything from ¼in to ½in (6mm to 1.3cm) apart and can be as many or as few as desired. The colour of the thread will usually match the colour of the fabric you are quilting. You don't always have to use a straight stitch, so experiment with a decorative, wavy, triple, or even a candlewicking or entredeaux stitch.

The easiest way to echo quilt is simply to guide the edge of the presser foot or walking foot against the edge of the shape you are echoing for the first line and then guide the edge of the presser foot against the last sewn line for the next one and continuing like this. However, if you want to be a little more precise, there are two techniques you can use, as follows.

Method A: At each pivot point, draw a line that bisects the angle. As you sew around the shape, when you pivot on this line you will be the correct distance away from the next edge. This will work at whatever distance you are away from the original shape.

Method B: To be really fussy, you can mark on your pivot lines how far apart you want the lines to be. They are usually the same distance apart, but why not try gradually widening the distance between the lines the farther out you go? Marking them like this will keep everything even, which is important if you are sewing to the edge of a block and want the same number of lines all around your design.

13

Celtic Square Templates
A quarter of the template is supplied

INSET SHAPE 1 *
CUT 8

INSET SHAPE 2 *
CUT 4

INSET SHAPE 3
CUT 4 *

INSET SHAPE 4 *
CUT 4

Clematis Square

This section describes the making and quilting of the Clematis Square.
Refer to the *Floral Dimensions* book for instructions on making the
clematis flowers, tulip flowers and central chrysanthemum.

Requirements
- Fabric: for tulip stems, tulip leaves, clematis stems, clematis flowers,
  frayed centres of the clematis flowers, two shades for the tulips, the
  large centre ruched flower and the small centre flower
- Machine sewing thread: cotton or polyester to match your fabrics
- Thin decorative cord or embroidery thread: for creating tendrils
- Toy stuffing: small pieces
- Fusible interfacing: 12in (30.5cm) square approximately
- Steam-A-Seam fusible web: 12in (30.5cm) square approximately
- Wool: for stuffing the stems
- Background fabric: 14in (35.5cm) square
- Wadding (batting): 14in (35.5cm) square
- Backing and sashing fabric

Start by tracing the design onto the right side of the background fabric.

Clematis Stems
Cut four bias strips 1in (2.5cm) wide x 5in (12.7cm) long and make the four stems. Blind hem stitch them in place. Stuff each stem with one strand of trapunto wool or similar.

Tendrils
Sew the tendrils to the background by either couching or chain stitching them. For more information on how to sew these, refer to the **Floral Dimensions** book. The thread tails at the bottom of the tendrils will be hidden under the flowers.

Clematis Flowers
Refer to the **Floral Dimensions** book to make the four clematis flowers and their frayed centres and sew these to the background following the pattern for the placement.

Tulip Flowers
Refer to the **Floral Dimensions** book to make the leaves, stems and tulip flowers and sew these to the background.

Chrysanthemum Flower
Follow the instructions in the **Floral Dimensions** book to make the ruched and scrunched chrysanthemum with the picot edge centre. Sew this to the background, making sure it covers the ends of the stems.

Finishing the Square
1 Pin the appliquéd square to the wadding and backing to make your quilting sandwich. If you are going to use my 'back-to-front' method to join the squares together you will need to follow the instructions for making up in the Back-to-Front Joining Technique section (Layering the Appliquéd Squares before Quilting), to ensure that the backing is marked correctly at this point.

2 I have used three different quilting patterns on the squares – crosshatching, parallel lines and echo quilting. I crosshatched this square, which is marked as follows. Using an easily removable marker draw a line 1in (2.5cm) in from each edge, resulting in a 12in (30.5cm) square. If you are using my back-to-front technique then these will be the tacking (basting) lines. Mark every 1in (2.5cm) along each of these lines, beginning and ending at a corner. Join the marks with diagonal lines. Skip over areas that have appliqué shapes – you won't be quilting across these.

3 Pin or tack (tack (baste) the layers together securely.

4 Choose the threads to quilt the squares. Cotton or rayon would be best, although a polyester one could be used. The colour should match closely with the fabric. I used the same 40 weight rayon in the top and in the bobbin. A different shade could be used in the bobbin but check the tension carefully to make sure you don't see any of the bottom thread on the top or the top thread on the bottom.

5 Use a quilting machine needle if you have one and a walking foot. Make sure you start with thread tails and adjust your machine to a stitch length 3.0. If your top and bottom threads match then you can 'fix' or secure the stitches at the beginning but leave thread tails. This means lots of ends to pull through and bury but gives a much better result than cutting them off. If the two threads are different shades, using the fix function may result in blobs of the top colour showing on the back. If you choose not to use the fix function, you will have to pull the threads through to the back, knot them and bury the ends. Use an easy-threading needle to save time.

6 When you reach an appliqué shape where the quilting line continues on the other side, fix the stitch (if using), lift the presser foot and pull out the top and bottom thread about 4in (10.2cm) to the side of the machine with your index finger. When these threads are cut in half, this will leave them long enough to pull through and bury. Move the fabric and position the needle on the other side of the appliqué shape at the beginning of the next line and continue as before.

7 Bury the thread tails after sewing a few lines. If you leave them all to the end, they are likely to get sewn in and be really difficult to separate.

8 This step is optional. Quilt around the outside of all flowers and leaves – quilting in the ditch of these motifs will create an attractive outline of them on the back of the quilt. You may need to use a narrow presser foot or zipper foot in some areas rather than the walking foot.

Clematis Square Templates

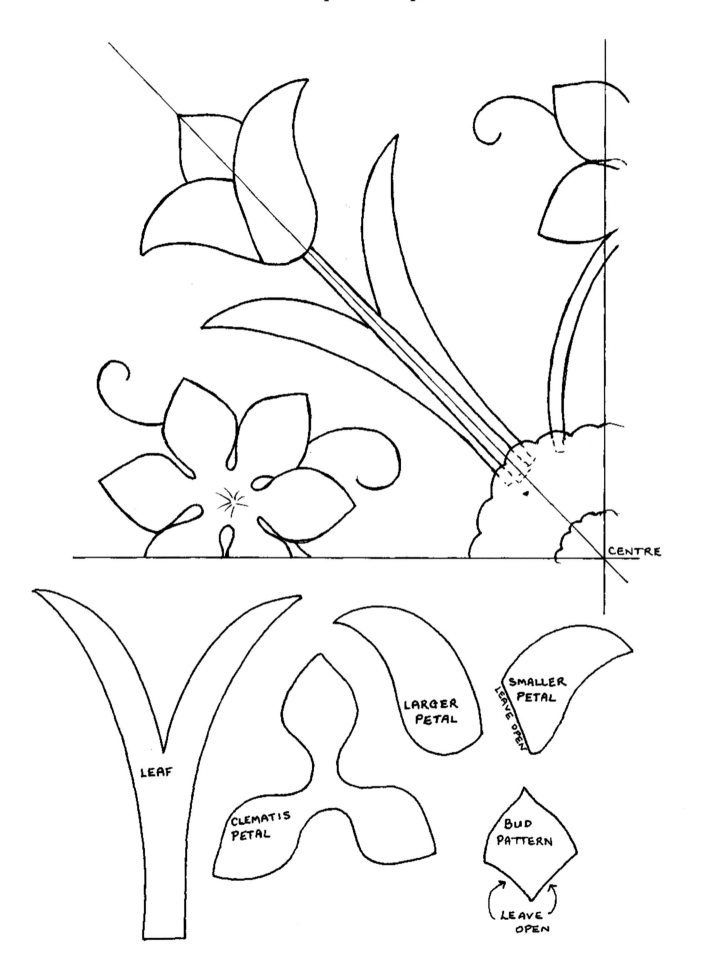

CENTRE

LEAF

CLEMATIS PETAL

LARGER PETAL

SMALLER PETAL

LEAVE OPEN

BUD PATTERN

LEAVE OPEN

Cyclamen Square

This section describes the making and quilting of the Cyclamen Square.
Refer to the *Floral Dimensions* book for instructions on making the
cyclamen flower, cyclamen bud, cyclamen leaves and marigold flower.

Requirements
- Fabric: for stems, leaves, cyclamen, circles, circle stems and centre flower
- Machine sewing thread: cotton or polyester to match above fabrics
- Machine sewing thread: rayon, cotton or polyester for satin stitching the leaves
- Tear-away stabiliser: small piece
- Wool: for stuffing stems
- Steam-A-Seam or Bondaweb fusible web
- Heatproof template plastic or Mylar 'Perfect Circles' (optional)
- Fasturn tube turner (optional)
- Background fabric: 14in (35.5cm) square.
- Wadding: 14in (35.5cm) square and small amount for stuffing the circles
- Backing and sashing fabric
- Fabric glue stick and Clover Fabric Folding Pen (optional)

Start by tracing the design onto the right side of the background fabric.

Cyclamen Stems

1 Cut four bias strips, 1⅛in x 4½in (2.8cm x 11.4cm) and four bias strips 1in x 3½in (2.5cm x 8.9cm). Fold each strip in half lengthways, right sides together. Sew a ¼in (6mm) seam along the side of the smaller strips and along the side and one end of the larger strips (Fig 1).

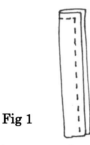

Fig 1

2 Clip the seam allowances at the corners of the larger strips and turn all of the tubes through to the right side using a tube turner or the needle and thread technique described in the **Floral Dimensions** book in the General Techniques section.

3 Stuff the large stems with two strands of thick wool and the smaller ones with one strand. You can do this easily with a Fasturn gadget by placing the wool in the top of the tube before pulling it through. Alternatively, use the 'cradle' method, as follows. Fold a length of thread in half and thread the loop through the eye of a blunt needle (see Fig 2A). Bring the thread ends around the needle and knot them (Fig 2B). Thread a length of wool that is twice as long as a large stem through the loop of thread, with the middle of the wool next to the loop (Fig 2C). Push the needle through the open end of one of the large stems, pulling the wool through with it. Bring the needle out through the top of the stem and cut off the thread that formed the cradle. Repeat for the other large stems. For the narrow stems, use a length of wool that is the same length as the stem and just place the end through the loop (Fig 3).

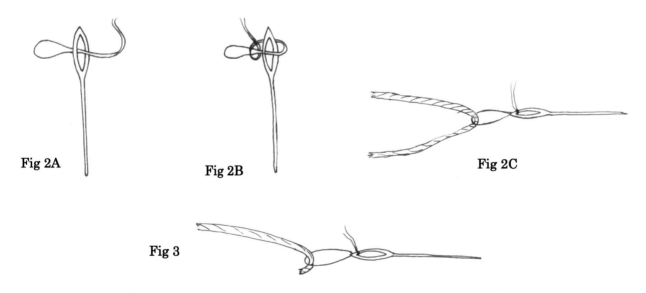

Fig 2A

Fig 2B

Fig 2C

Fig 3

Cyclamen Petals

Follow the directions in the **Floral Dimensions** book for making the five petals for each of the four cyclamen flowers – twenty in all. Sew these onto the larger stems and then to the background as described in the book, following the pattern for the placement.

Cyclamen Bud

Follow the directions in the **Floral Dimensions** book for making the five petals for each of the four cyclamen buds – twenty in all. Sew these onto the smaller stems but don't sew the buds to the background until after the square has been quilted.

Leaves

1 Draw twelve of the leaf shapes, Template 4, on to Steam-A-Seam fusible web. Make sure you draw them on the backing paper that has the web attached and then rough cut them out. Peel off the backing paper that isn't drawn on.

2 Place the web side of the Steam-A-Seam shapes to the wrong side of your chosen leaf fabric. Press with an iron and cut the leaves out on the lines. Peel off the second backing paper.

3 Place a piece of wadding behind each leaf and then trim it approximately ¼in (6mm) from the edge of the leaf fabric. Refer to the pattern for placement and iron the four Leaf 1 shapes in place.

4 Satin stitch around the edge. Sew a triple stitch along the vein lines. Repeat for the four Leaf 2 shapes and then the four Leaf 3 shapes.

Circle Stems

Cut four bias strips, 1in x 4in (2.5cm x 10.2cm) to make four bias stems. On the background fabric, refer to the pattern and mark the placement of the stems. Use a fabric glue stick or pins to secure the stems to the background and then sew them using a blind hem stitch or similar. Stuff the stems using wool or cord.

Circles

Cut out a ⅝in (1.5cm) diameter circle from either Mylar heatproof template plastic, thin card or use the equivalent size from a 'Perfect Circles' pack. Draw around the template on the wrong side of your fabric. Use Method A or Method B below to prepare the fabric circles. Make twelve circles in all and hand stitch them in place after the square has been quilted.

Method A: Sew a gathering stitch (length 3.0) approximately ⅛in (3mm) from the edge of the paper circle. Use an open-toe foot, don't fix the beginning and end and leave thread tails (Fig 4A). Keeping the thread tails away from the scissors, trim each circle about ⅛in (3mm) from the stitching line (Fig 4B). If you want to add a little padding under the circles, then cut out circles of wadding the same size as your finished circles. Place the wadding circle, if used, in the centre of the wrong side of the fabric circle and your template on top. Knot the thread tails that are on the wrong side and pull up the threads on the right side tightly (Fig 4C). Spray starch, remove the template and press again.

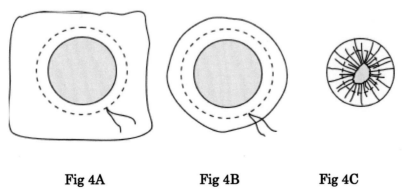

Fig 4A   Fig 4B   Fig 4C

Method B: For this method, cut your fabric approximately ⅛in–¼in (3mm–6mm) from the drawn line and then place the heatproof template in the centre on the wrong side. Apply a Clover Fabric

Folding Pen to the fabric edge and then a Sewline Glue Stick. Using the side edge of a mini iron or small iron, press the fabric edge over the top of the template. When all the edges have been turned, remove the template plastic and press again. Place a slightly smaller circle of wadding underneath the circle before appliquéing to the background if desired.

Marigold Centre
Follow the directions in the **Floral Dimensions** book to make the marigold with a frayed centre.

Finishing the Square
1 Pin the appliquéd square to the wadding and backing to make your quilting sandwich. If you are going to use my 'back-to-front' method to join the squares together you will need to follow the instructions for making up in the Back-to-Front Joining Technique section (Layering the Appliquéd Squares before Quilting), to ensure that the backing is marked correctly at this point.

2 I have used three different quilting patterns on the squares – crosshatching, parallel lines and echo quilting. I crosshatched this square which is marked as follows. Using an easily removable marker draw a line 1in (2.5cm) in from each edge, resulting in a 12in (30.5cm) square. If you are using my back-to-front technique then these will be the tacking (basting) lines. Mark every 1in (2.5cm) along each of these lines, beginning and ending at a corner. Join the marks with diagonal lines. Skip over areas that have appliqué shapes – you won't be quilting across these.

3 Pin or tack (tack (baste) the layers together securely. Choose the threads to quilt the squares. Cotton or rayon would be best, although a polyester could be used. The colour should match closely with the fabric. I used the same 40 weight rayon in the top and the bobbin. A different shade could be used in the bobbin but check the tension to make sure you don't see any of the bottom thread on the top or the top thread on the bottom.

4 Use a quilting machine needle if you have one and a walking foot. Make sure you start with thread tails and adjust your machine to a stitch length 3.0. If your top and bottom threads match then you can 'fix' or secure the stitches at the beginning but leave thread tails. This means lots of ends to pull through and bury but gives a much better result than cutting them off. If the two threads are different shades, using the fix function may result in blobs of the top colour showing on the back. If you choose not to use the fix function, you will have to pull the threads through to the back, knot them and bury the ends. Use an easy-threading needle to save time.

5 When you reach an appliqué shape where the quilting line continues on the other side, fix the stitch (if using), lift the presser foot and pull out the top and bottom thread about 4in (10.2cm) to the side of the machine using your index finger. When these threads are cut in half, this will leave them long enough to pull through and bury. Move the fabric and position the needle the other side of the appliqué shape at the beginning of the next line and continue as before.

6 Bury the thread tails after sewing a few lines. If you leave them all to the end, they are likely to get sewn in and be really difficult to separate.

7 This step is optional. Quilt around the outside of all flowers and leaves – quilting in the ditch of these motifs will create an attractive outline of them on the back of the quilt. You may need to use a narrow presser foot or zipper foot in some areas rather than the walking foot.

8 Following the pattern for placement, hand sew the cyclamen buds in place, then the circles and then the centre marigold flower. Sew the frayed centre to the middle of the marigold flower.

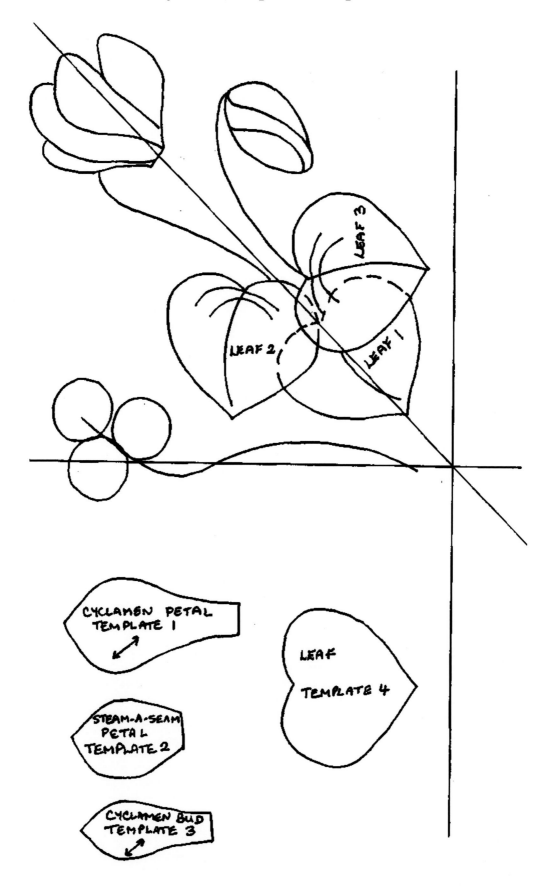

CYCLAMEN PETAL
TEMPLATE 1

STEAM-A-SEAM
PETAL
TEMPLATE 2

CYCLAMEN BUD
TEMPLATE 3

LEAF
TEMPLATE 4

LEAF 3

LEAF 2

LEAF 1

Dresden Plate Square

This section describes the making and quilting of the central square of the quilt. Refer to the *Floral Dimensions* book for instructions on making the daffodil flowers, stems and leaves and the carnation flowers, stems and leaves.

Requirements
- Fabric: for the inner background, daffodils, carnations, stems, leaves and centre
- Machine sewing thread: cotton or polyester to match your fabrics
- Rayon, polyester or cotton thread: for satin stitching around the inner background, the centre, the carnations and leaves
- Embroidery cotton (floss), or similar: for daffodil stamens, about 4½yd (4m)
- Stuffing: small piece
- Background fabric: 14in (35.5cm) square
- Wadding: 14in (35.5cm) square
- Backing and sashing fabric
- Solvy water soluble stabilizer or similar

Dresden Plate Background

1 On the wrong side of the fabric, draw around the Pointed Segment and the Rounded Segment four times each and cut them out on the line.

2 Sew them together, alternating the shapes, using ¼in (6mm) seams. Iron the seams open.

3 On the Steam-A-Seam, draw around the two Dresden Segment Tops, four times each and cut them out on the line.

4 Peel the backing paper off and iron them to the tops of the fabric segments on the wrong side. Peel off the second backing paper.

5 Mark or crease the centre lines of the 14in (35.5cm) background square and place the Dresden Segments centrally on top so that the pointed segments are pointing towards the corners of the square. Carefully iron in place.

6 Satin stitch around the outside of the Dresden Plate, width 3.0. Don't forget to use tear-away stabiliser underneath.

Daffodils

Follow the directions in the **Floral Dimensions** book to make four daffodil flowers with stems and leaves. Sew these in place on the Dresden Plate segments with the rounded tops – one on each.

Carnations

Follow the directions in the **Floral Dimensions** book to make the leaves, stems and flowers of the four carnations. Sew on each of the four Dresden Plate segments with the pointed tops.

Gazania Centre

1 Make a plastic template of the two shapes for the large centre.

2 On the wrong side of your fabric, draw Shape 1 eight times and cut them out on the line.

3 Draw the seam lines and the two marks onto the wrong side of each shape.

4 Pin two shapes, right sides together. Select a straight stitch, length 2.0 without a 'fix' or locking stitch. Sew from the top edge down to the first mark (which is about ¼in from the top) on the seam line and then press the reverse button on the machine. Sew backwards to the top edge, release the reverse button, sew one stitch forward and then 'fix' or lock the stitch (Fig 1). Remove the fabric from the machine and cut the threads. Iron the seam open.

Fig 1

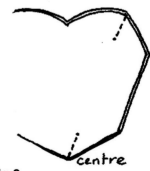

Fig 2

5 Turn the shape around and repeat step 4, starting from the centre edge (Fig 2).

25

6 Sew the other three pairs together in the same way.

7 Next, sew two of the pairs together and then the two halves together in the same way (sew the two sides separately – do not sew all the way across). The middle seam will sit on top of the ones at the sides – see Photo 1 and Photo 2.

Photo 1   Photo 2

8 Using the smaller template, Shape 2, cut out eight shapes from the fabric that will be behind the window. 'Fussy cut' these if desired.

9 Machine sew these to the seam allowances of the shape you just made so that the right sides will be facing out through the windows. Use a stitch length 3.0 and secure the beginning and end stitches. See Photo 3 and Photo 4.

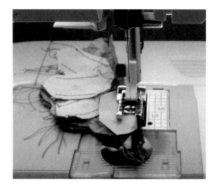

Photo 3   Photo 4

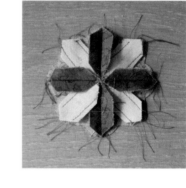

10 Clip only the very point at the centre end of the windows, to allow it to lie flat. Trim all thread ends.

11 Pin a piece of wadding underneath, a little larger than the centre. Fold back the folded edges and hand or machine sew them back, creating a window effect (Photo 5).

Photo 5

12 For the small circle on top, on the wrong side of the fabric, draw around the larger of the two circles. Machine or hand sew a gathering stitch on the line and then cut the fabric approximately ¼in (6mm) from this line.

13 Use a Mylar circle or make your own from heatproof plastic the same size as the smaller of the two circles. Place this in the centre of the wrong side of the larger circle and pull up the gathering threads tightly. Spray starch and then iron.

14 Remove the template. Cut a circle of wadding slightly smaller than the circle template and place it inside.
Photo 6 shows the finished flower.

Photo 6

Finishing the Square

1 Pin the 14in (35.5cm) square of wadding behind the background square and stitch in the ditch of the Dresden petals using a feather stitch or similar.

2 Trim the wadding that is under the large centre so that it is just under the edge. Pin this to the centre of the Dresden petals. Place tear-away stabiliser underneath and sew the centre to the background with a small zigzag stitch, using tweezers to tuck the thread ends under. Now satin stitch, width 3.0, over the zigzag stitching.

3 Sew the small centre to the large one using a small buttonhole appliqué stitch.

4 Pin the appliquéd square to the backing to make your quilting sandwich. If you are going to use my 'back-to-front' method to join the squares together you will need to follow the instructions for making up in the Back-to-Front Joining Technique section (Layering the Appliquéd Squares before Quilting), to ensure that the backing is marked correctly at this point. Quilt the square using your own choice of background quilting. I chose to echo quilt mine as follows. Echo quilting is the term used for stitching that echoes the shape of an appliquéd or quilted design, similar to ripples on a pond. The lines are anything from ¼in to ½in (6mm to 1.3cm) apart and can be as many or as few as desired. The colour of the thread will usually match the colour of the fabric you are quilting. The easy way is to simply guide the edge of the presser foot or walking foot against the edge of the shape you are echoing for the first line and then guide the edge of the presser foot against the last sewn line for the next one and continuing like this. However, if you want to be a little more precise, there are two techniques you can use, as follows.

Method A: At each pivot point, draw a line that bisects the angle. As you sew around the shape, when you pivot on this line you will be the correct distance away from the next edge. This will work at whatever distance you are away from the original shape.

Method B: To be really fussy, you can mark on your pivot lines how far apart you want the lines to be. They are usually the same distance apart, but why not try gradually widening the distance between the lines the farther out you go. Marking them like this will keep everything even, which is important if you are sewing to the edge of a block and want the same number of lines all around your design.

5 Finish by straight stitch quilting in the Dresden segment seam ditches and around the satin stitching.

Dresden Plate Square Templates

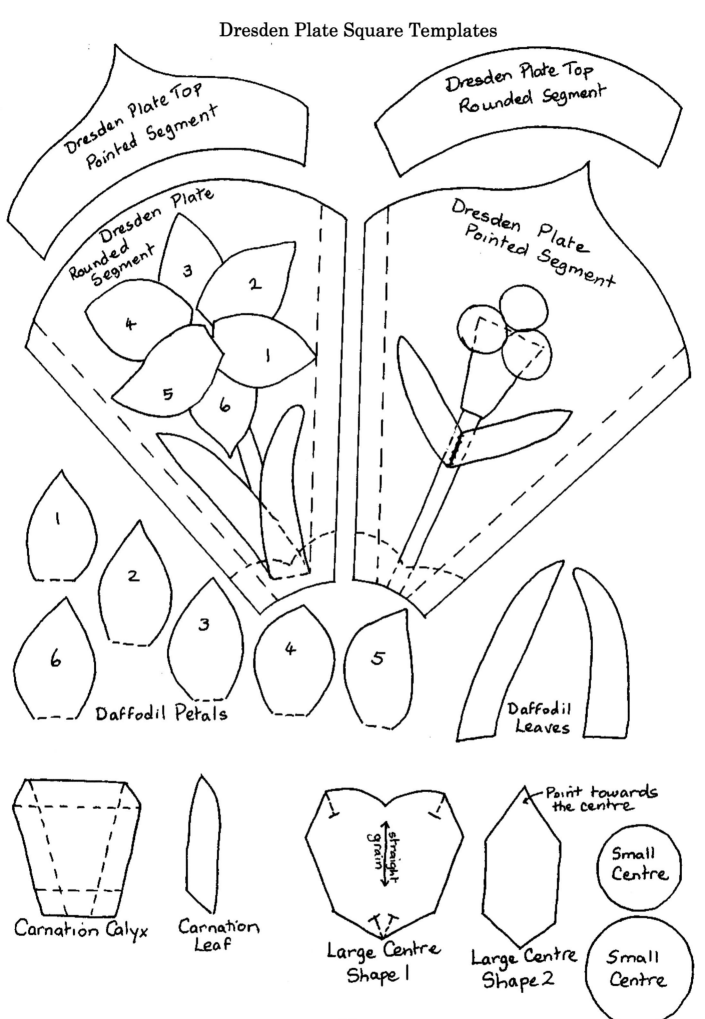

Dresden Plate Top Pointed Segment

Dresden Plate Top Rounded Segment

Dresden Plate Rounded Segment

Dresden Plate Pointed Segment

3
2
4
1
5
6

Daffodil Petals

1
2
6
3
4
5

Daffodil Leaves

Carnation Calyx

Carnation Leaf

straight grain

Large Centre Shape 1

Point towards the centre

Large Centre Shape 2

Small Centre

Small Centre

Foxglove Square

This section describes the making and quilting of the Foxglove Square.
Refer to the *Floral Dimensions* book for instructions on making the
foxgloves and gerbera.

Requirements
- Fabric: for the stems, leaves, centre flower, the outsides, insides and the tops
  of the foxgloves
- Machine sewing thread: cotton or polyester to match your fabrics
- Rayon, polyester or cotton thread: for satin stitching around the edge of the
  foxgloves and leaves
- Background fabric: 14in (35.5cm) square
- Wadding: 14in (35.5cm) square
- Backing and sashing fabric
- Bias bars ¼in (6mm) and $^3/_{16}$in (5mm)
- Steam-A-Seam fusible web: 18in (46cm) square approximately
- Water-soluble stabiliser (Solvy): 12in (30.5cm) square approximately
- Cord or wool: to stuff stems
- Embroidery hoop (optional)
- Covered button (optional)

Foxglove Stems

Cut four bias strips 1⅛in x 4in (2.8cm x 10.2cm) to make four bias stems. On the background fabric, refer to the pattern and mark the placement of the stems. Use a fabric glue stick or pins to secure the stems to the background and then sew them using a blind hem stitch or similar. Stuff the stems using wool or cord. If required, refer to the **Floral Dimensions** book for using bias bars to make stems.

Stems and Leaves

1 Cut eight bias strips each 1in x 5in (2.5cm x 12.7in) and make eight bias stems.

2 Draw four of each of the leaf shapes (1R, 2R, 3R, 4R) on Steam-A-Seam (on the backing paper that has the web attached), making sure they are all pointing in the same direction. Rough cut around the outside of the drawing.

3 Peel off the backing paper that hasn't been drawn on and place the leaves, web side down, on the wrong side of the fabric so they are on the bias grain. Press with an iron and cut the leaves out on the lines.

4 On the background fabric, mark the placement of leaves 2 and 3. Remove the backing paper, iron these in place and satin stitch, width 2.0, around the edges.

5 On the background fabric, mark the placement of the stems that have three leaves. Sew these to the background using a blind hem stitch. Stuff with wool if desired. Repeat for the other stems.

6 Satin stitch the remaining leaves in place. Sew a triple stitch vein down the centre of each leaf.

Foxgloves

Refer to the instructions in the **Floral Dimensions** book to make the foxgloves. Sew the foxgloves to the background, placing the pairs of large petals over the stems so the tops are 4in (10.2cm) from the centre, the tops of the medium ones are 5in (12.7cm) from the centre and the tops of the smaller pairs are 6in (15.2cm) from the centre.

Foxglove Calyx

Place two pieces of fabric approximately 4in (10.2cm) square, right sides together. On the wrong side of the fabric, draw around the calyx shape four times, leaving about ½in (1.3cm) between them. With a stitch length 1.5, sew around the shapes on the lines. Cut around the outside of the stitching, leaving about ⅛in (3mm) seam allowance. Make a small slit in the back and turn each shape through to the right side and press flat with an iron. Sew one calyx to the top of each foxglove using either a buttonhole appliqué stitch or blind hem stitch along the top and sides only.

Gerbera

From the centre flower fabric, cut a bias strip 2¼inx 15½in (5.7cm x 39.4cm) and follow the directions in the **Floral Dimensions** book to make the large ruched flower.

Finishing the Square

1 Pin the appliquéd square to the wadding and backing to make your quilting sandwich. If you are going to use my 'back-to-front' method to join the squares together you will need to follow the instructions for making up in the Back-to-Front Joining Technique section (Layering the Appliquéd Squares before Quilting), to ensure that the backing is marked correctly at this point.

2 I have used three different quilting patterns on the squares – crosshatching, parallel lines and echo quilting. I crosshatched this square which is marked as follows. Using an easily removable marker draw a line 1in (2.5cm) in from each edge, resulting in a 12in (30.5cm) square. If you are using my back-to-front technique then these will be the tacking (basting) lines. Mark every 1in (2.5cm) along each of these lines, beginning and ending at a corner. Join the marks with diagonal lines. Skip over areas that have appliqué shapes – you won't be quilting across these.

3 Pin or tack (tack (baste) the layers together securely.

4 Choose the threads to quilt the squares. Cotton or rayon would be best, although a polyester one could be used. The colour should match closely with the fabric. I used the same 40 weight rayon in the top and the bobbin. A different shade could be used in the bobbin but check the tension carefully to make sure you don't see any of the bottom thread on the top or the top thread on the bottom.

5 Use a quilting machine needle if you have one and a walking foot. Make sure you start with thread tails and adjust your machine to a stitch length 3.0. If your top and bottom threads match then you can 'fix' or secure the stitches at the beginning but leave thread tails. This means lots of ends to pull through and bury but gives a much better result than cutting them off. If the two threads are different shades, using the fix function may result in blobs of the top colour showing on the back. If you choose not to use the fix function, you will have to pull the threads through to the back, knot them and bury the ends. Use an easy-threading needle to save time.

6 When you reach an appliqué shape where the quilting line continues on the other side, fix the stitch (if using), lift the presser foot and using your index finger, pull out the top and bottom thread about 4in (10.2cm) to the side of the machine. When these threads are cut in half, this will leave them long enough to pull through and bury. Move the fabric and position the needle the other side of the appliqué shape at the beginning of the next line and continue as before.

7 Bury the thread tails after sewing a few lines. If you leave them all to the end, they are likely to get sewn in and be really difficult to separate.

8 This step is optional. Quilt around the outside of all flowers and leaves – quilting in the ditch of these motifs will create an attractive outline of them on the back of the quilt. You may need to use a narrow presser foot or zipper foot in some areas rather than the walking foot.

9 Hand sew the gerbera to the centre of the square by stitching between the petals. Finish by hand sewing a small covered button in the centre if desired.

Foxglove Square Templates

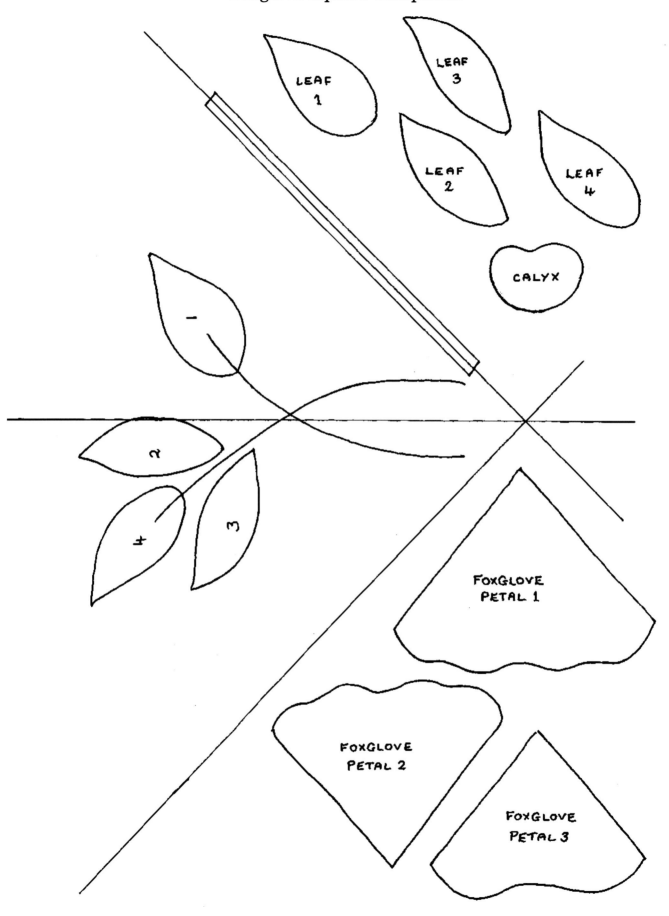

LEAF 1

LEAF 3

LEAF 2

LEAF 4

CALYX

FOXGLOVE PETAL 1

FOXGLOVE PETAL 2

FOXGLOVE PETAL 3

Fuchsia Square

This section describes the making and quilting of the Fuchsia Square.
Refer to the *Floral Dimensions* book for instructions on making the
fuchsia and primrose flowers and the berry clusters.

Requirements
- Fabric: for stems and circle, leaves, berries, small flowers, inside and outside fuchsias
- Machine sewing thread: cotton or polyester to match your fabrics
- Rayon, polyester or cotton thread: for satin stitching around the leaves
- Decorative cord: for tendrils and fuchsia stamens
- Stuffing: small piece
- Three small buttons plus fabric to cover them: for primrose centres
- Mylar plastic templates, 'Perfect Circles' templates or thin card
- Wool: to stuff stems and circle (optional)
- Background fabric: 14in (35.5cm) square
- Wadding: 14in (35.5cm) square
- Backing and sashing fabric

Fuchsias

Follow the instructions in the *Floral Dimensions* book to make the four fuchsia flowers and place these to one side.

Tendrils

Using the template and an easily removable marker, mark the tendrils, stems and leaves on to the background fabric. Sew the tendrils to the background by either couching or chain stitching them. For more information on how to sew these, refer to the *Floral Dimensions* book. The thread tails at the bottom of the tendrils will be hidden under the stem.

Stems

1 Cut 1in (2.5cm) wide bias strips in a total length of 22in (60cm). Make stems 1, 2 and 3 marked on the template and then blind hem them in place. Stuff the stems with wool or cord if desired.

2 From the remaining bias strip/s, cut three lengths, two 4in (10.2cm) and one 7in (17.8cm) for stems 4, 5 and 6. On each of these, turn ¼in (6mm) hem, wrong sides together, at one short end (see Fig 1). Make these into stems as before.

Fig 1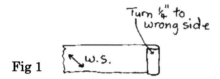

3 Using a needle with a large eye, thread the cords that are at the top of three of the fuchsias through the finished end of the stems and out through the top. Place a pin at the end to prevent it from slipping through.

4 Pin the cords at the top of fuchsia A to the background, with the bottom of the flower pointing upwards and the top about ¼in (6mm) above the line that marks the centre of the stem – see Photo 1. Sew the cords to the line using a triple stitch.

Photo 1

5 Blind hem stitch stems 4, 5 and 6 in place and either hand sew or blind hem the top of the fuchsias to the end of the stems. Fuchsia A will be flipped over the stem (see Photo 2) and the other three fuchsias secured to the background after the square has been quilted.

Photo 2

Circle Stem

Cut a 1⅛in (2.8cm) wide bias strip in a total length of 30in (76cm) and make this into a stem. Iron the stem into a curve before using a fabric glue to place it on the background. Begin and end the stem where the leaf 1 will go. Blind hem stitch in place. Stuff with wool if desired. To prevent the large circle from puckering when you are stuffing it, bring the needle with the wool through to the back every few inches and either leave a loop or cut it. This will provide a little 'give' and enable the circle to lie flat.

Leaves

Trace the leaf shapes on Steam-A-Seam fusible web, on the side that has the web attached, and rough cut them out. Peel off the backing paper that has not been drawn on and iron them to the wrong side of the fabric you are using for the leaves. Cut the leaves out on the line. Peel off the second backing paper and place the leaves in position on the background. The X marks the base of each leaf. Satin stitch, width 2.0, using a matching thread.

To sew the veins, mark a line down the centre of each leaf from the base and ending about ¼in (6mm) from the point. Machine a triple stitch on the line from the base to about halfway and then change to a single stitch for the remainder. This will give the effect of a thicker vein at the base getting narrower towards the point.

Primroses

Refer to the **Floral Dimensions** book to make the three primrose flowers. The seam edges can be turned under when the flowers are sewn to the background after the square has been quilted.

Berries

Make nine berries by following the instructions in the **Floral Dimensions** book. Sew these to the background after the square has been quilted.

Finishing the Square

1 Pin the appliquéd square to the wadding and backing to make your quilting sandwich If you are going to use my 'back-to-front' method to join the squares together you will need to follow the instructions for making up in the Back-to-Front Joining Technique section (Layering the Appliquéd Squares before Quilting), to ensure that the backing is marked correctly at this point.

2 I have used three different quilting patterns on the squares – crosshatching, parallel lines and echo quilting. I crosshatched this square which is marked as follows. Using an easily removable marker draw a line 1in (2.5cm) in from each edge, resulting in a 12in (30.5cm) square. If you are using my back-to-front technique then these will be the tacking (basting) lines. Mark every 1in (2.5cm) along each of these lines, beginning and ending at a corner. Join the marks with diagonal lines. Skip over areas that have appliqué shapes – you won't be quilting across these.

3 Pin or tack (tack (baste) the layers together securely.

4 Choose the threads to quilt the squares. Cotton or rayon would be best, although a polyester one could be used. The colour should match closely with the fabric. I used the same 40 weight rayon in the top and the bobbin. A different shade could be used in the bobbin but check the tension carefully to make sure you don't see any of the bottom thread on the top or the top thread on the bottom.

5 Use a quilting machine needle if you have one and a walking foot. When you are quilting the background, move the fuchsias out of the way as needed.

6 Make sure you start with thread tails and adjust your machine to a stitch length 3.0. If your top and bottom threads match then you can 'fix' or secure the stitches at the beginning but leave thread tails. This means lots of ends to pull through and bury but gives a much better result than cutting them off. If the two threads are different shades, using the fix function may result in blobs of the top colour showing on the back. If you choose not to use the fix function, you will have to pull the threads through to the back, knot them and bury the ends. Use an easy-threading needle to save time.

7 When you reach an appliqué shape where the quilting line continues on the other side, fix the stitch (if using), lift the presser foot and pull out the top and bottom thread about 4in (10.2cm) to the side of the machine. When these threads are cut in half, this will leave them long enough to pull through and bury. Move the fabric and position the needle the other side of the appliqué shape at the beginning of the next line and continue as before.

8 Bury the thread tails after sewing a few lines. If you leave them all to the end, they are likely to get sewn in and be really difficult to separate.

9 This step is optional. Quilt around the outside of all flowers and leaves – quilting in the ditch of these motifs will create an attractive outline of them on the back of the quilt. You may need to use a narrow presser foot or zipper foot in some areas rather than the walking foot.

10 Hand sew the backs of two of the outer petals of each fuchsia to the background to keep them in place. Hand sew the berries and small flowers to the background.

11 Finish by covering three small buttons and sewing them to the centres of the primroses.

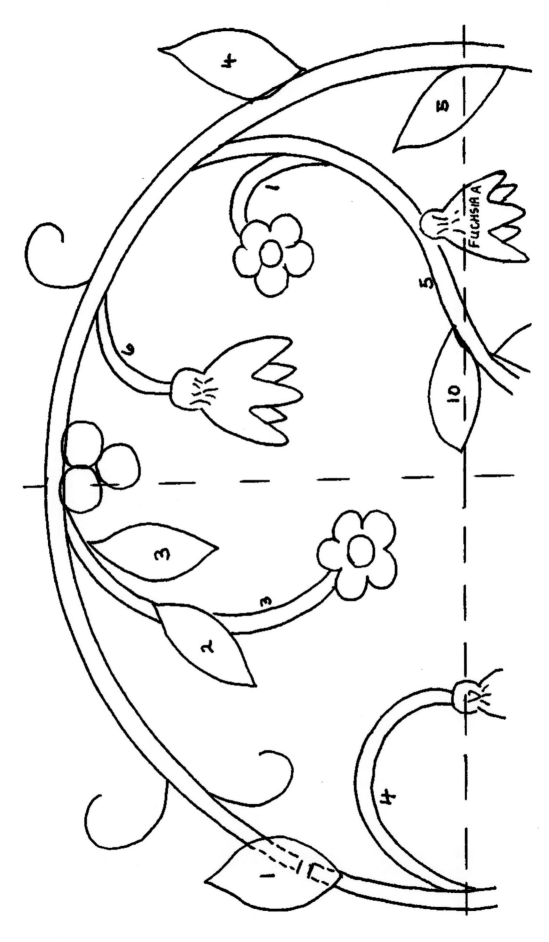

Fuchsia Templates

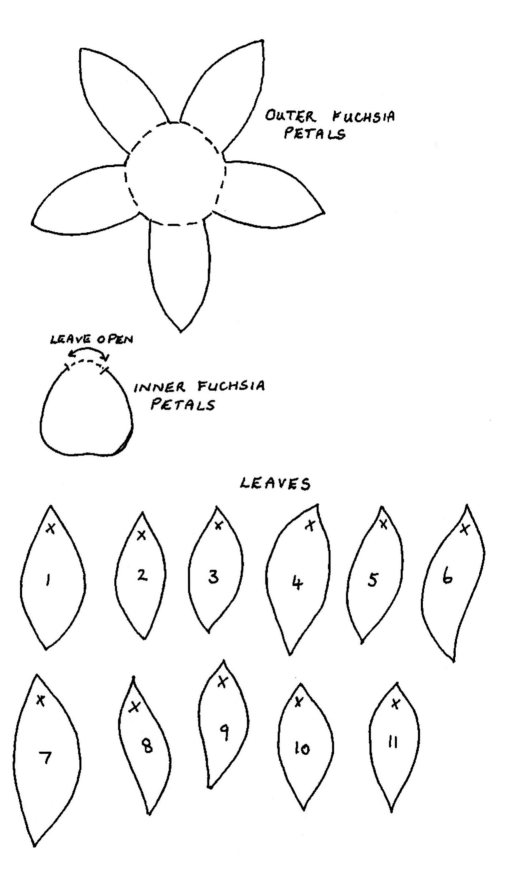

OUTER FUCHSIA PETALS

LEAVE OPEN

INNER FUCHSIA PETALS

LEAVES

1 2 3 4 5 6

7 8 9 10 11

Hawaiian Square

This section describes the making and quilting of the Hawaiian Square.
Refer to the *Floral Dimensions* book for instructions on making the
passion flower in the centre.

Requirements
- Fabric: for the main Hawaiian shape (12in/30.5cm square), the windows, large centre flower, small centre flower and the background of the centre flowers
- Machine sewing thread: cotton or polyester to match your fabrics
- Background fabric: 14in (35.5cm) square
- Wadding (batting): 14in (35.5cm) square
- Backing and sashing fabric
- Steam-A-Seam fusible web: 12in square approximately
- Fray Check liquid
- Clover Fabric Folding Pen or spray starch (optional)

Hawaiian Shape

1 Draw two diagonal lines on the Steam-A-Seam from corner to corner and then trace the pattern a quarter at a time onto the paper side that has the web attached.

2 Cut the shape out on the outside and inside lines.

3 Peel the backing paper off and finger press and then iron the web side of the Steam-A-Seam to the wrong side of the appliqué fabric. Apply a drop of Fray Check to each inside point and sharp inside curves.

4 Cut the appliqué fabric about ¼in 96mm) away from the edges of the pattern. Clip the inside points and the sharp inside curves.

5 Turn the raw edges over the Steam-A-Seam edge using your preferred method as described in the **Floral Dimensions** book.

The Windows

1 Place the window fabric, right side up and the Hawaiian shape on top. Draw around the inside and outside of each window shape, except the centre one. Remove the Hawaiian shape and then cut out the window fabric between the inside and outside window shapes. This will make the window fabric a little larger than the hole but not so large that it shows around the outside of the hole. Cut the centre window fabric a little larger than the hole.

2 Remove the backing paper carefully and press the edges back over the web, ironing only the very edge (otherwise the web will stick to the iron!) – see Photo 1 and Photo 2.

Photo 1   Photo 2

3 Press the window fabric shapes to the back of the Hawaiian shape so that the right side of the fabric shows through the windows.

4 On the right side, using an easily removable marker, draw a diagonal line from corner to corner in both directions on the 14in (35.5cm) square of background fabric. Mark the centre of each side and join the opposite ones.

5 Place the Hawaiian shape on the right side of the background centrally, lining up the diagonal lines and the lines at the side.

6 Machine appliqué around the shape using a blind hem or buttonhole stitch.

Passion Flower

Follow the instructions in the **Floral Dimensions** book to make the passion flower and then hand sew this to the centre of the Hawaiian square.

Finishing the Square

Pin the appliquéd square to the wadding and backing to make your quilting sandwich. If you are going to use my 'back-to-front' method to join the squares together you will need to follow the instructions for making up in the Back-to-Front Joining Technique section (Layering the Appliquéd Squares before Quilting), to ensure that the backing is marked correctly at this point. Quilt the square with your own choice of background quilting. I chose to echo quilt mine (described below). Echo quilting is the term used for stitching that echoes the shape of an appliquéd or quilted design, similar to ripples on a pond (see the detail pictures below). The lines are anything from ¼in to ½in (6mm to 1.3cm) apart and can be as many or as few as desired. The colour of the thread will usually match the colour of the fabric you are quilting. You don't always have to use a straight stitch, so experiment with a decorative, wavy, triple, or even a candlewicking or entredeaux stitch.

The easiest way to echo quilt is to guide the edge of the presser foot or walking foot against the edge of the shape you are echoing for the first line. For the next line, guide the edge of the presser foot against the last sewn line and continue like this. However, if you want to be a little more precise, there are two techniques you can use, as follows.

Method A: At each pivot point, draw a line that bisects the angle. As you sew around the shape, when you pivot on this line you will be the correct distance away from the next edge. This will work at whatever distance you are away from the original shape.

Method B: To be really fussy, you can mark on your pivot lines how far apart you want the lines to be. They are usually the same distance apart, but why not try gradually widening the distance between the lines the farther out you go. Marking them like this will keep everything even, which is important if you are sewing to the edge of a block and want the same number of lines all around your design.

Hawaiian Square Template
A quarter of the template is supplied

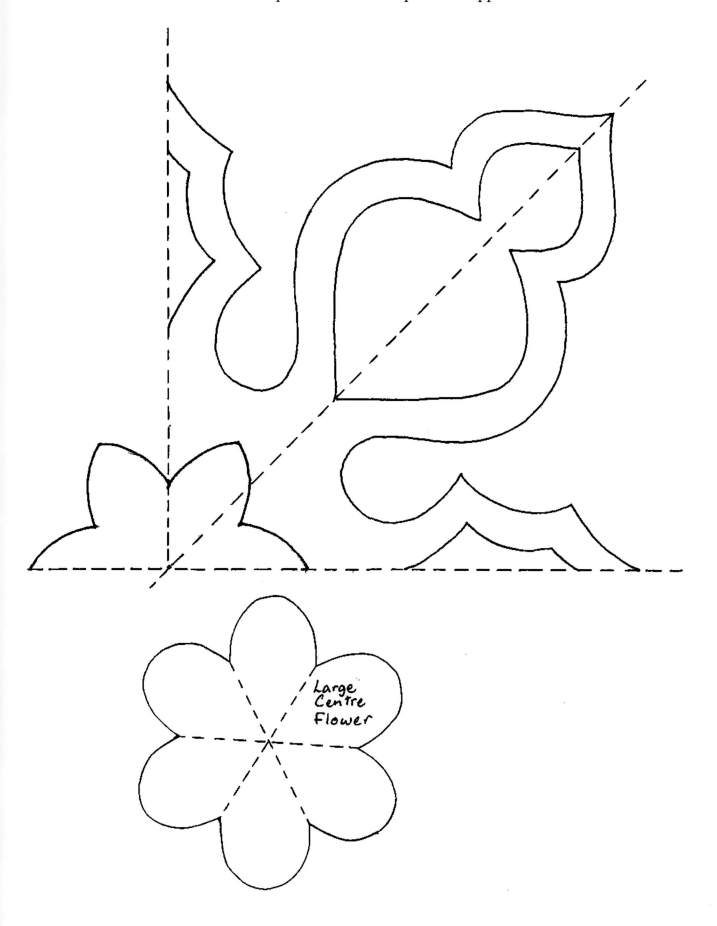

Large
Centre
Flower

Lily of the Valley Square

This section describes the making and quilting of the Lily of the Valley Square. Refer to the *Floral Dimensions* book for instructions on making the lily of the valley flower and the grape clusters and leaves.

Requirements

- Fabric: for the grape vine, grape vine leaves, lily stem, lily leaves, lilies and grapes
- Machine sewing thread: cotton or polyester to match your fabrics
- Rayon, polyester or cotton thread: for satin stitching around the edge of the grape vine leaves
- Wool: for stuffing stems
- Decorative cord: for creating tendrils
- Background fabric: 14in (35.5cm) square
- Wadding (batting): 14in (35.5cm) square and some small pieces
- Stuffing: small pieces
- Backing and sashing fabric
- Medium-weight fusible interfacing: 12in (30.5cm) square approximately
- Spray starch
- Steam-A-Seam fusible web
- Mylar plastic templates, 'Perfect Circles' templates or thin card
- Needle with large eye: for sewing cords to the back

Using an easily removable marker, copy the pattern onto the right side of the background square. Only the centre of the vine needs to be marked as your lines will then be hidden.

Tendrils
Sew the tendrils to the background by either couching or chain stitching them. For more information on how to sew these, refer to the **Floral Dimensions** book. The thread tails at the bottom of the tendrils will be hidden under the stem.

Grape Vine and Lily Stem
1 Cut 1⅛in (2.8cm) wide bias strips to a total length of approximately 50in (127cm) and make the stems for the vine.

2 Iron the vine in a curved shape before placing it over the lines, following the lettered order on the pattern where indicated. You can butt the ends of shorter lengths of vine strips underneath where a leaf will be sewn. Make sure all ends will be covered by another stem or leaf.

3 Sew the vine to the background using a blind hem stitch or similar stitch.

4 Cut a bias strip 1in x 6in (2.5cm x 15.2cm) for the lily stem and repeat the steps above, making sure that the end is long enough to be hidden under the leaves.

5 Stuff the vine with two lengths of wool and the lily stem with one length. To prevent the large circle from puckering when you are stuffing it, bring the needle with the wool through to the back every few inches and either leave a loop or cut it. This will provide a little 'give' and enable the circle to lie flat.

Lily Leaves
1 Draw the two leaf shapes on to the wrong side of the fabric.

2 Place the right side of the fabric on the non-sticky side of some fusible interfacing. Sew on the drawn line, leaving a gap where marked on the smaller leaf but sewing all the way round on the larger leaf.

3 On both leaves, cut the fabric and the fusible interfacing about ¼in (6mm) from the stitching line and clip all curves and points.

4 On the large leaf, make a slit approximately 1in (2.5cm) in the centre of the interfacing and turn through to the right side. Turn the smaller leaf to the right side through the gap. Press both leaves flat so that the interfacing sticks to the wrong side of the fabric.

5 Place the leaves over a piece of wadding and sew the accent lines.

6 Trim the wadding just underneath the edge of the leaves. Pin the leaves to the background and sew in place using blind hem stitch.

Vine Leaves
1 Trace the four leaf shapes on a piece of Steam-A-Seam on the backing paper that has the web attached and then rough cut them out.

2 Peel off the backing paper that was not drawn on and then iron the leaf shapes to the wrong side of the fabric. Cut the leaves out on the line.

3 Peel off the second backing paper and place the leaves in position on the background. Satin stitch, width 2.0, using a matching thread.

4 Pin a piece of wadding under each leaf on the wrong side of the background fabric and triple stitch the vein lines, length 3.0. Sew a straight stitch next to the satin stitching on the inside only. On the back, trim the wadding close to the straight stitching that is on the inside of the satin stitching.

Grapes

Make twenty-six grapes following the instructions in the *Floral Dimensions* book.

Lily of the Valley Flowers

Make seven of these following the instructions in the *Floral Dimensions* book.

Finishing the Square

1 Pin the appliquéd square to the wadding and backing to make your quilting sandwich. If you are going to use my 'back-to-front' method to join the squares together you will need to follow the instructions for making up in the Back-to-Front Joining Technique section (Layering the Appliquéd Squares before Quilting), to ensure that the backing is marked correctly at this point.

2 I have used three different quilting patterns on the squares – crosshatching, parallel lines and echo quilting. I crosshatched this square, which is marked as follows. Using an easily removable marker, draw a line 1in (2.5cm) in from each edge, resulting in a 12in (30.5cm) square. If you are using my back-to-front technique then these will be the tacking (basting) lines. Mark every 1in (2.5cm) along each of these lines, beginning and ending at a corner. Join the marks with diagonal lines. Skip over areas that have appliqué shapes – you won't be quilting across these.

3 Pin or tack (tack (baste) the layers securely. Choose the threads to quilt the squares. Cotton or rayon would be best, although a polyester one could be used. The colour should match closely with the fabric. I used the same 40 weight rayon in the top and the bobbin. A different shade could be used in the bobbin but check the tension carefully to make sure you don't see any of the bottom thread on the top or the top thread on the bottom. Use a quilting machine needle if you have one and a walking foot.

4 Make sure you start with thread tails and adjust your machine to a stitch length 3.0. If your top and bottom threads match then you can 'fix' or secure the stitches at the beginning but leave thread tails. This means lots of ends to pull through and bury but gives a much better result than cutting them off. If the two threads are different shades, using the fix may result in blobs of the top colour showing on the back. If you choose not to use the fix function, you will have to pull the threads through to the back, knot them and bury the ends. Use an easy-threading needle to save time.

5 When you reach an appliqué shape where the quilting line continues on the other side, fix the stitch (if using), lift the presser foot and with your index finger, pull out the top and bottom thread about 4in (10.2cm) to the side of the machine. When these threads are cut in half, this will leave them long enough to pull through and bury. Move the fabric and position the needle the other side of the appliqué shape at the beginning of the next line and continue as before.

6 Bury the thread tails after sewing a few lines. If you leave them all to the end, they are likely to get sewn in and be really difficult to separate.

7 This step is optional. Quilt around the outside of all the stems and leaves – quilting in the ditch of these motifs will create an attractive outline of them on the back of the quilt. You may need to use a narrow presser foot or zipper foot in some areas rather than the walking foot.

8 Hand sew the grapes and the lily of the valley flowers to the square to finish.

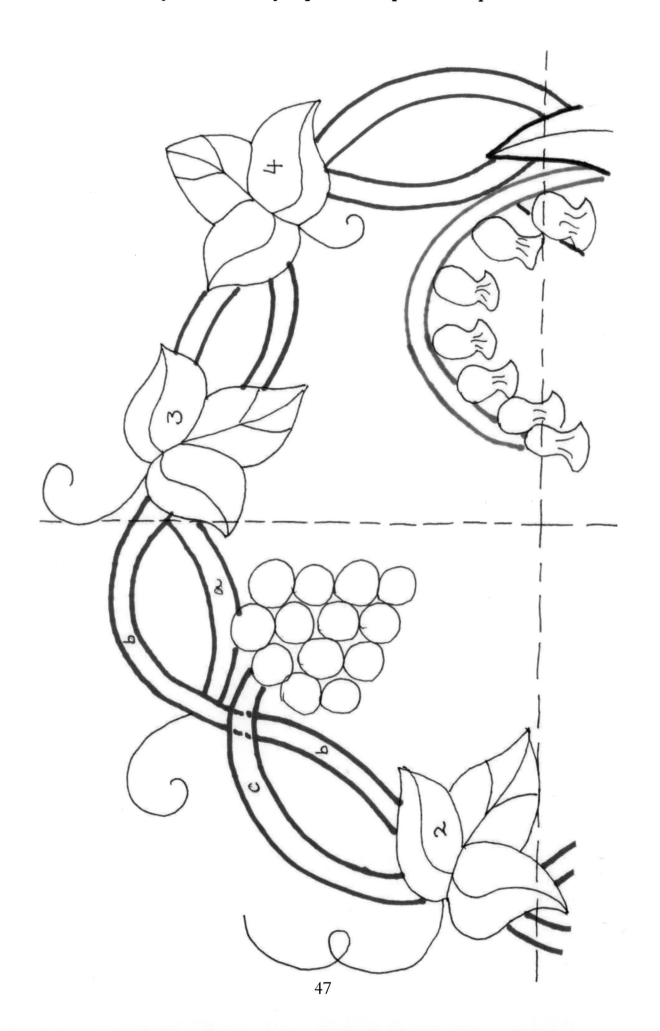

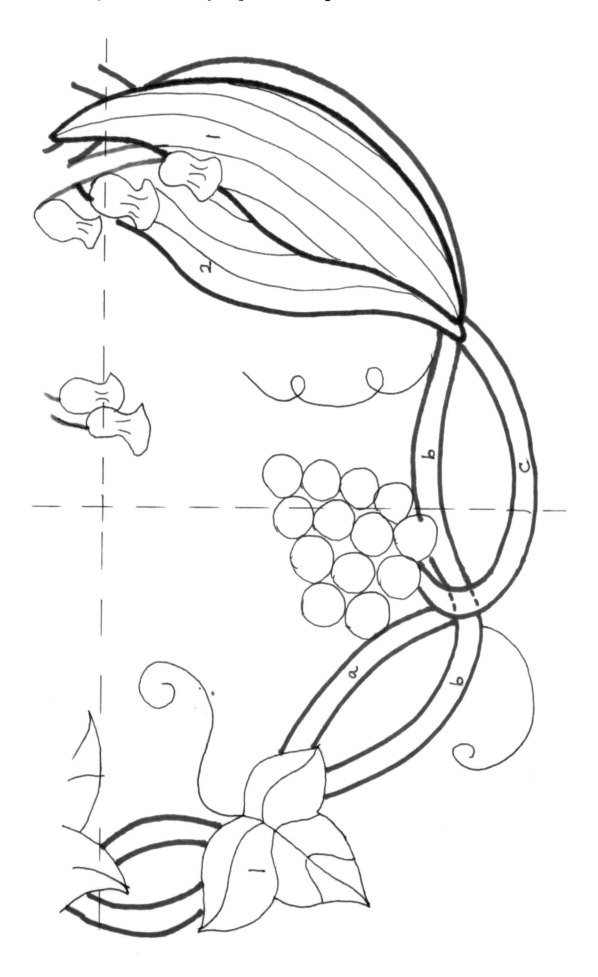

Lily of the Valley Square Templates – leaves

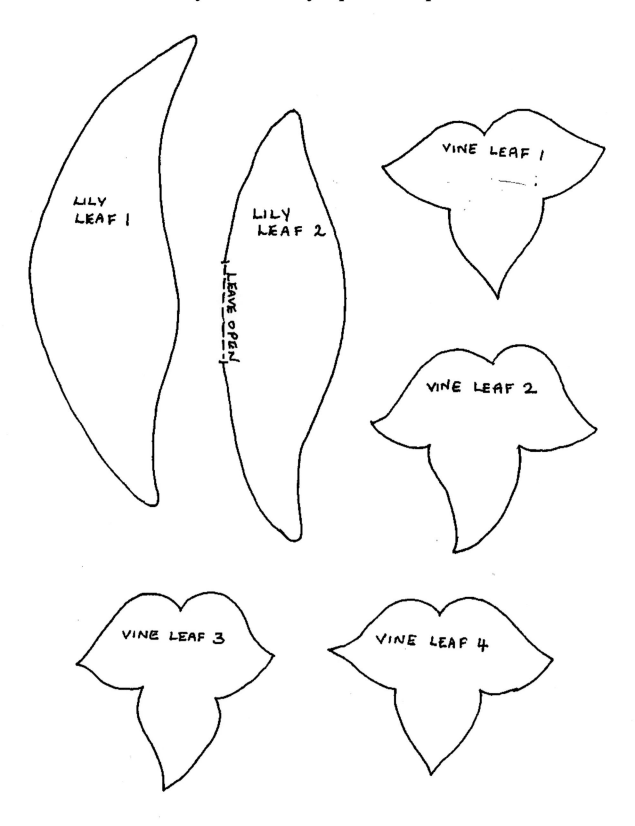

LILY LEAF 1

LILY LEAF 2

LEAVE OPEN

VINE LEAF 1

VINE LEAF 2

VINE LEAF 3

VINE LEAF 4

Pansy Square

This section describes the making and quilting of the Pansy Square. Refer to the *Floral Dimensions* book for instructions on making the pansy flowers, lily, bell flowers and leaves.

Requirements
- Fabric: for the stems, leaves, lily, pansies, bells, and flower shape at base of circle
- Machine sewing thread: cotton or polyester to match your fabrics
- Rayon, polyester or cotton thread: for veins on pansies and satin stitching around the edge of the flower shape and small leaves
- Decorative cord: for stamens in lily
- Beads: for centres of bell flowers, stamens on lily and pansy centres
- Fusible interfacing: 12in (30.5cm) square approximately
- Steam-A-Seam 2 fusible web or Bondaweb
- Wadding (batting): 14in (35.5cm) square and some small pieces
- Background fabric: 14in (35.5cm) square
- Backing and sashing fabric
- Fray Check seam sealant

Small Stems and Circular Stem

1 On the background fabric, mark the placement of the circular stems and small stems. Only the centre of these needs to be marked as your line will then be hidden.

2 Cut 1in (2.5cm) wide bias strips in a total length of approximately 16in (40.6cm) and make the small stems.

3 Sew the small stems to the background using a blind hem stitch. Make sure you sew the shorter ones first (marked 'a' on the template) so that the ends will be covered by the longer ones (marked 'b').

4 Cut 1¼in (3.2cm) wide bias strips in a total length of 28in (71cm). Make the circular stem and press it in a curved shape before placing it over the line on the background. You can butt the ends of shorter lengths underneath where a leaf or flower will be sewn. Blind hem stitch in place. Stuff the stem with wool if desired.

Small Leaves

1 Trace the small leaf shape six times on the Steam-A-Seam (the side that has the web attached) and rough cut them out.

2 Peel off the backing paper that is not drawn on and iron the shapes to the wrong side of the fabric. Cut the leaves out on the line.

3 Peel off the backing paper and place the leaves in position on the background. Satin stitch, width 1.5, around the edges using a matching thread.

Large Leaves

1 Trace the large leaf shape four times onto Steam-A-Seam and then cut them out on the line.

2 Peel off the backing paper and iron the leaves to the wrong side of the fabric, leaving about 1in (2.5cm) between each leaf for turnings. Cut the fabric about ³⁄₁₆in (5mm) from the edge of the Steam-A-Seam.

3 Place a drop of Fray Check at each indent and when dry, clip the fabric right up to the point of each indent.

4 Turn the edges over the Steam-A-Seam using your preferred method (see step 3 of Turning Raw Edges to the Wrong Side in the General Techniques section of the ***Floral Dimensions*** book).

5 Carefully remove the second backing paper and then press the edges again.

6 Pin and then tack (baste) the shapes to a piece of wadding. Trim the wadding away just under the edges of the leaves.

7 Blind hem stitch the leaves to the background. Sew a triple stitch down the centre of each leaf to represent the vein.

Flower at the Base

1 Trace the shapes for the flower (templates labelled 'Centre', 'Petal A', 'Petal B' and 'Petal C' and 'Petal D') on Steam-A-Seam (the side that has the web attached) and rough cut them out.

2 Peel off the backing paper that is not drawn on and iron on to the wrong side of the fabric. Cut the shapes out on the line.

3 Peel off the second backing paper and place Petal A and Petal B on the background first. Satin stitch them to the background, width 2.0. Next place Petal C and Petal D in position and satin stitch them in place. Finally, satin stitch the centre on top of Petals C and D.

Lily Flower

Follow the instructions in the *Floral Dimensions* book to make the lily at the top of the square. Sew this in place on the background.

Pansy Flowers

There are two different designs for the pansies, A and B, and four petal shapes for each of the designs. Petal Shape 2 forms two of the petals. Two of the Pansy A designs are reversed (AR) and two of the Pansy B designs are reversed (BR). Follow the instructions for making the pansies in the *Floral Dimensions* book and then sew them in place on the background.

Bell Flowers

Make the eight bells by referring to the instructions in the *Floral Dimensions* book. Sew these to the background after the square has been quilted.

Finishing the Square

1 Pin the appliquéd square to the wadding and backing to make your quilting sandwich. If you are going to use my 'back-to-front' method to join the squares together you will need to follow the instructions for making up in the Back-to-Front Joining Technique section (Layering the Appliquéd Squares before Quilting), to ensure that the backing is marked correctly at this point.

2 I have used three different quilting patterns on the squares – crosshatching, parallel lines and echo quilting. I crosshatched this square, which is marked as follows. Using an easily removable marker, draw a line 1in (2.5cm) in from each edge, resulting in a 12in (30.5cm) square. If you are using my back-to-front technique then these will be the tacking (basting) lines. Mark every 1in (2.5cm) along each of these lines, beginning and ending at a corner. Join the marks with diagonal lines. Skip over areas that have appliqué shapes – you won't be quilting across these.

3 Pin or tack (tack (baste) the layers securely.

4 Choose the threads to quilt the squares. Cotton or rayon would be best, although a polyester one could be used. The colour should match closely with the fabric. I used the same 40 weight rayon in the top and the bobbin. A different shade could be used in the bobbin but check the tension carefully to make sure you don't see any of the bottom thread on the top or the top thread on the bottom. Use a quilting machine needle if you have one and a walking foot.

5 Make sure you start with thread tails and adjust your machine to a stitch length 3.0. If your top and bottom threads match then you can 'fix' or secure the stitches at the beginning but leave thread tails. This means lots of ends to pull through and bury but gives a much better result than cutting them off. If the two threads are different shades, using the fix may result in blobs of the top colour showing on the back. If you choose not to use the fix function, you will have to pull the threads through to the back, knot them and bury the ends. Use an easy-threading needle to save time.

6 When you reach an appliqué shape where the quilting line continues on the other side, fix the stitch (if using), lift the presser foot and using your index finger, pull out the top and bottom thread about 4in (10.2cm) to the side of the machine. When these threads are cut in half, this will leave them long enough to pull through and bury. Move the fabric and position the needle the other side of the appliqué shape at the beginning of the next line and continue as before.

7 Bury the thread tails after sewing a few lines. If you leave them all to the end, they are likely to get sewn in and be really difficult to separate.

8 This step is optional. Quilt around the outside of all flowers and leaves – quilting in the ditch of these motifs will create an attractive outline of them on the back of the quilt. You may need to use a narrow presser foot or zipper foot in some areas rather than the walking foot.

9 Hand sew the bell flowers to the square after quilting is finished.

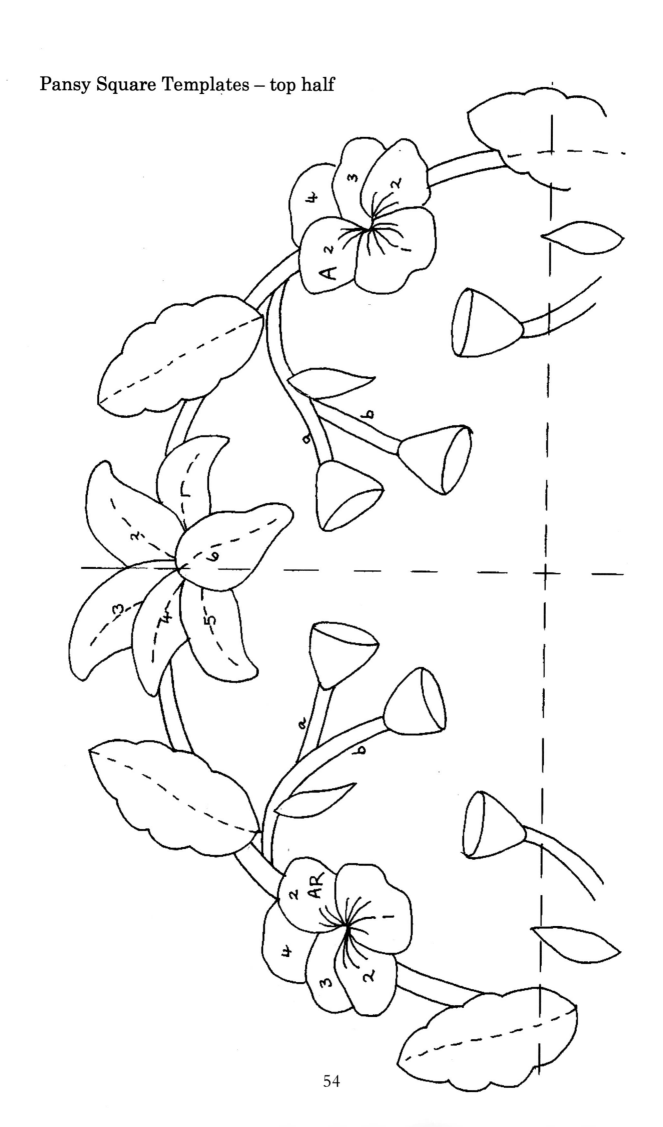

Pansy Square Templates – bottom half

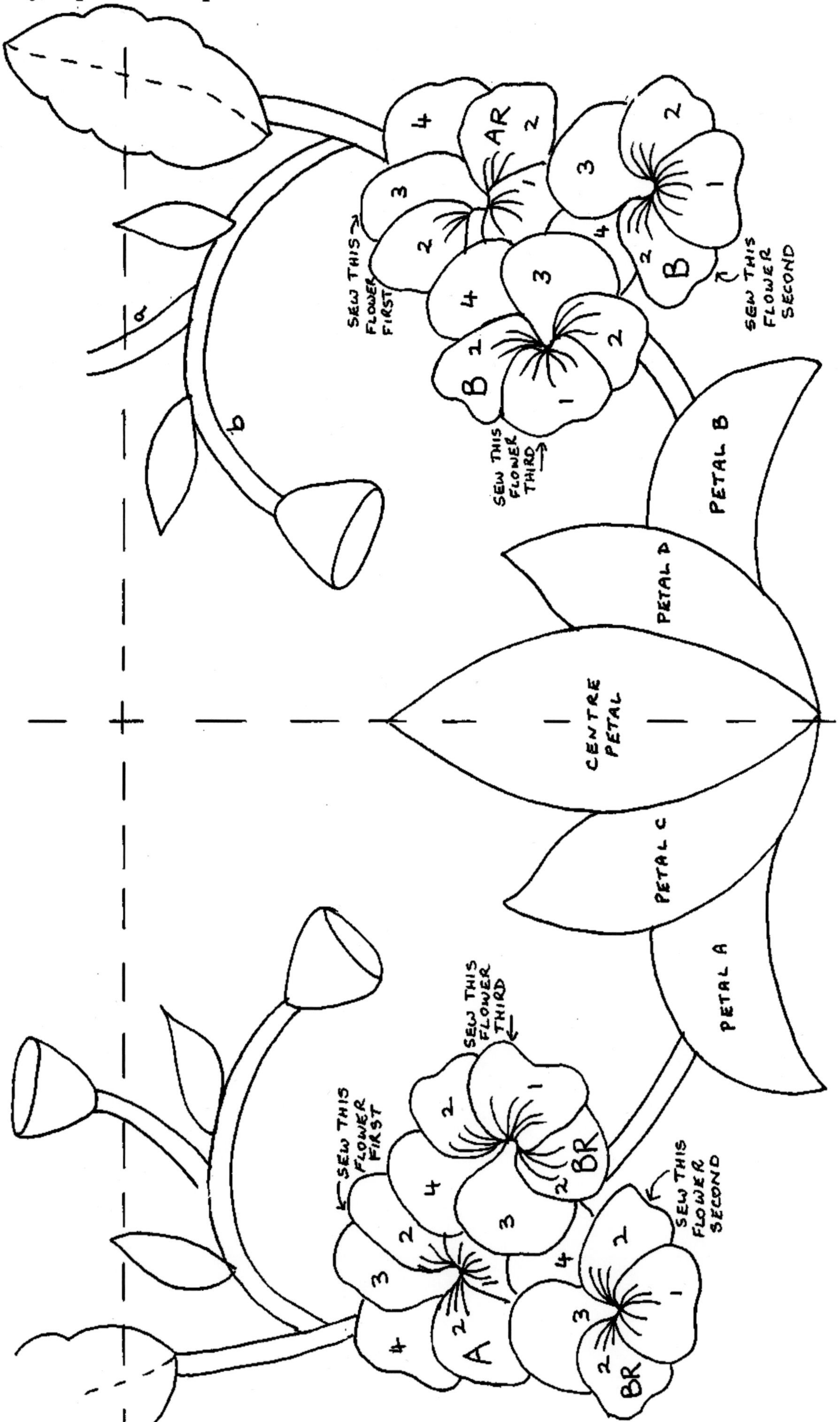

SEW THIS FLOWER FIRST

SEW THIS FLOWER SECOND

SEW THIS FLOWER THIRD

AR

B

B

PETAL B

PETAL D

CENTRE PETAL

PETAL C

PETAL A

SEW THIS FLOWER FIRST

SEW THIS FLOWER SECOND

SEW THIS FLOWER THIRD

BR

A

BR

Pansy Square Templates

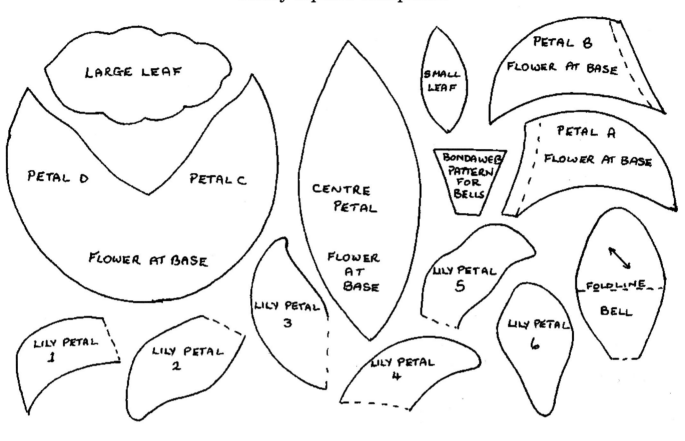

LARGE LEAF

PETAL D   PETAL C

FLOWER AT BASE

CENTRE PETAL

FLOWER AT BASE

SMALL LEAF

BONDAWEB PATTERN FOR BELLS

PETAL B FLOWER AT BASE

PETAL A FLOWER AT BASE

LILY PETAL 5

FOLD LINE BELL

LILY PETAL 6

LILY PETAL 3

LILY PETAL 4

LILY PETAL 1

LILY PETAL 2

PANSY PETALS

A 1

A 2

A 3

A 4

AR 1

AR 2

AR 3

AR 4

B 1

B 2

B 3

B 4

BR 1

BR 2

BR 3

BR 4

Rose Square

This section describes the making and quilting of the Rose Square. Refer to the *Floral Dimensions* book for instructions on making the rose flowers, rosebuds and leaves.

Requirements

- Fabric: for the stems, leaves, roses, rosebuds and small circle
- Machine sewing thread: cotton or polyester to match your fabrics
- Rayon, polyester or cotton thread: for satin stitching around the leaves
- Cord or wool: to stuff the stems
- Cord for tendrils
- Tracing paper: approximately two 5in (12.7cm) squares
- Steam-A-Seam fusible web
- Tear-away stabiliser
- Water-soluble stabiliser (Solvy) (optional)
- Mylar plastic templates, 'Perfect Circles' templates or thin card
- Wadding (batting): 14in (35.5cm) square and some small pieces for the leaves
- Background fabric: 14in (35.5cm) square
- Backing and sashing fabric
- Clover Fabric Folding Pen and fabric glue stick (optional)

Trace the design for the vine, stems and tendrils onto the front of the background fabric.

Large Leaves

1 On the side that has the web attached on a piece of Steam-A-Seam, draw around the large leaf shapes. Rough cut them out around the lines, peel off the backing paper and iron, web side down, to the wrong side of the leaf fabric.

2 Cut the fabric and Steam-A-Seam on the drawn lines.

3 Peel off the second backing paper and iron the two leaves to the background following the positioning on the pattern. Satin stitch, width 2.0 around the edge and then sew the leaf veins with a triple stitch.

Stems and Vine

1 Cut 1in (2.5cm) wide bias strips to a total length of 22in (56cm). Refer to Making Bias Stems in the General Techniques section of the *Floral Dimensions* book to make stems A, B, C, D, E, F and G marked on the pattern.

2 Blind hem stitch these stems in place (refer to Blind Hem Stitching Appliqué, in the General Techniques section of the *Floral Dimensions* book), starting with stem A, and making sure that stem C covers the end of stem A. Stuff the stems with wool or cord.

3 Cut 1⅛in (2.8cm) wide bias strips to a total length of 28in (71cm) and make these into strips for the vine.

4 Blind hem appliqué the vine to the background, making any joins under a flower, the large stem at the bottom or a bud. Make sure that the vine covers the end of stems D, E, F and G and that stem F covers the end of stem E. Stuff the vine with wool or cord. To prevent the vine from puckering, when you are stuffing it make a slit in the vine in the centre of where a rose, a bud or the stem at the bottom will be covering it. Bring the needle with the wool up through these slits and either leave a loop or cut the wool. This will provide a little 'give' and enable the vine to lie flat.

5 On Steam-A-Seam, draw around the pattern for stem H and cut it out on the line.

6 Peel off the backing paper and iron the web side to the wrong side of the stem fabric. Cut the fabric about ¼in (6mm) away from the edge of the Steam-A-Seam.

7 Turn the edges to the wrong side – refer to step 3 of Turning Raw Edges to the Wrong Side in the General Techniques section of the *Floral Dimensions* book. There is no need to turn the top edge at the narrower end as it will be under the small circle.

8 Remove the backing paper, finger press or iron the edges over and blind hem stitch in place.

Circle

Cut out a ⅝in (1.5cm) diameter circle from either Mylar heatproof template plastic, thin card or use the equivalent size from a 'Perfect Circles' pack. Draw around the template on the wrong side of your fabric. You can do this in one of two ways, as follows.

Method A: Sew a gathering stitch (length 3.0) approximately ⅛in (3mm) from the edge of the circle. Use an open-toe foot, don't fix the beginning and end and leave thread tails (see Fig 1). Keeping the thread tails away from the scissors, trim each circle about ⅛in (3mm) from the stitching line (Fig 2).

If you want to add a little padding under the circles, then cut out circles of wadding a little smaller than the size of your finished circles. Place the wadding circle, if used, in the centre of the wrong side of the fabric circle and your template on top. Knot the thread tails that are on the wrong side and pull up the threads on the right side tightly (Fig 3). Spray starch, remove the template and press again.

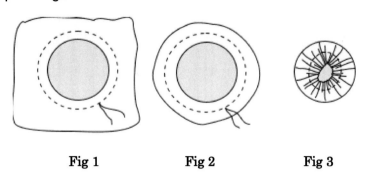

| Fig 1 | Fig 2 | Fig 3 |

Method B: For this method cut your fabric approximately ⅛in–¼in (3mm–6mm) from the drawn line and then place the heatproof template in the centre on the wrong side. Apply a Clover Fabric Folding Pen to the fabric edge and then a Sewline Glue Stick. Using the side edge of a mini iron or small iron, press the fabric edge over the top of the template. When all the edges have been turned, remove the template plastic and press again. Place a slightly smaller circle of wadding underneath the circle before appliquéing to the background if desired.

Tendrils
Sew the tendrils to the background by either couching or chain stitching them. For more information on how to sew these, refer to the **Floral Dimensions** book. The thread tails at the bottom of the tendrils will be hidden under the stem.

Small Leaves
1 On Steam-A-Seam, draw around each leaf shape using the pattern provided onto the paper side that has the web attached. You will need one A, one AR, two B, two BR and one C. Cut each leaf out on the line.

2 Peel off the backing paper and iron the Steam-A-Seam leaves to the wrong side of the fabric. Cut the fabric about ¼in (6mm) from the edge of the Steam-A-Seam for each leaf.

3 Turn the edges over the Steam-A-Seam edge. Peel off the backing paper and iron or finger press the edge over.

4 Tack (baste) each leaf to a piece of wadding and then trim the wadding just under the edge of the leaf.

5 Appliqué the leaves in position using the blind hem stitch or buttonhole appliqué stitch. Sew a triple stitch down the centre of each leaf to represent the vein.

Rosebuds
Make the seven rosebuds by following the directions in the **Floral Dimensions** book. Place the rosebuds in position on the background (use fabric glue to hold them) and sew a small zigzag stitch along the base and ¼in (6mm) up both sides to secure.

Calyx
Make a calyx for each of the buds following the instructions in the **Floral Dimensions** book and then sew them in position.

Roses

Refer to the **Floral Dimensions** book to make three roses, sewing them to the background as described in the book.

Finishing the Square

1 Pin the appliquéd square to the wadding and backing to make your quilting sandwich. If you are going to use my 'back-to-front' method to join the squares together you will need to follow the instructions for making up in the Back-to-Front Joining Technique section (Layering the Appliquéd Squares before Quilting), to ensure that the backing is marked correctly at this point.

2 I have used three different quilting patterns on the squares – crosshatching, parallel lines and echo quilting. I crosshatched this square, which is marked as follows. Using an easily removable marker, draw a line 1in (2.5cm) in from each edge, resulting in a 12in (30.5cm) square. If you are using my back-to-front technique then these will be the tacking (basting) lines. Mark every 1in (2.5cm) along each of these lines, beginning and ending at a corner. Join the marks with diagonal lines. Skip over areas that have appliqué shapes – you won't be quilting across these.

3 Pin or tack (tack (baste) the layers securely. Choose the threads to quilt the squares. Cotton or rayon would be best, although a polyester one could be used. The colour should match closely with the fabric. I used the same 40 weight rayon in the top and the bobbin. A different shade could be used in the bobbin but check the tension carefully to make sure you don't see any of the bottom thread on the top or the top thread on the bottom. Use a quilting machine needle if you have one and a walking foot.

4 Make sure you start with thread tails and adjust your machine to a stitch length 3.0. If your top and bottom threads match then you can 'fix' or secure the stitches at the beginning but leave thread tails. This means lots of ends to pull through and bury but gives a much better result than cutting them off. If the two threads are different shades, using the fix may result in blobs of the top colour showing on the back. If you choose not to use the fix function, you will have to pull the threads through to the back, knot them and bury the ends. Use an easy-threading needle to save time.

5 When you reach an appliqué shape where the quilting line continues on the other side, fix the stitch (if using), lift the presser foot and using your index finger, pull out the top and bottom thread about 4in (10.2cm) to the side of the machine. When these threads are cut in half, this will leave them long enough to pull through and bury. Move the fabric and position the needle the other side of the appliqué shape at the beginning of the next line and continue as before.

6 Bury the thread tails after sewing a few lines. If you leave them all to the end, they are likely to get sewn in and be really difficult to separate.

7 This step is optional. Quilt around the outside of all stems, leaves and flowers – quilting in the ditch of these motifs will create an attractive outline of them on the back of the quilt. You may need to use a narrow presser foot or zipper foot in some areas rather than the walking foot.

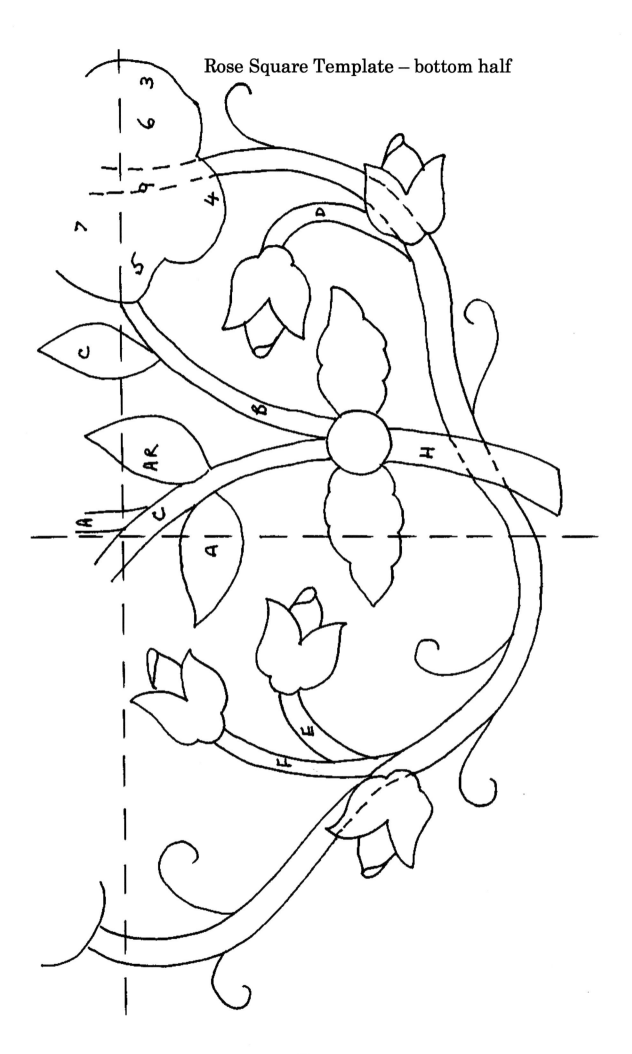

Rose Square Templates

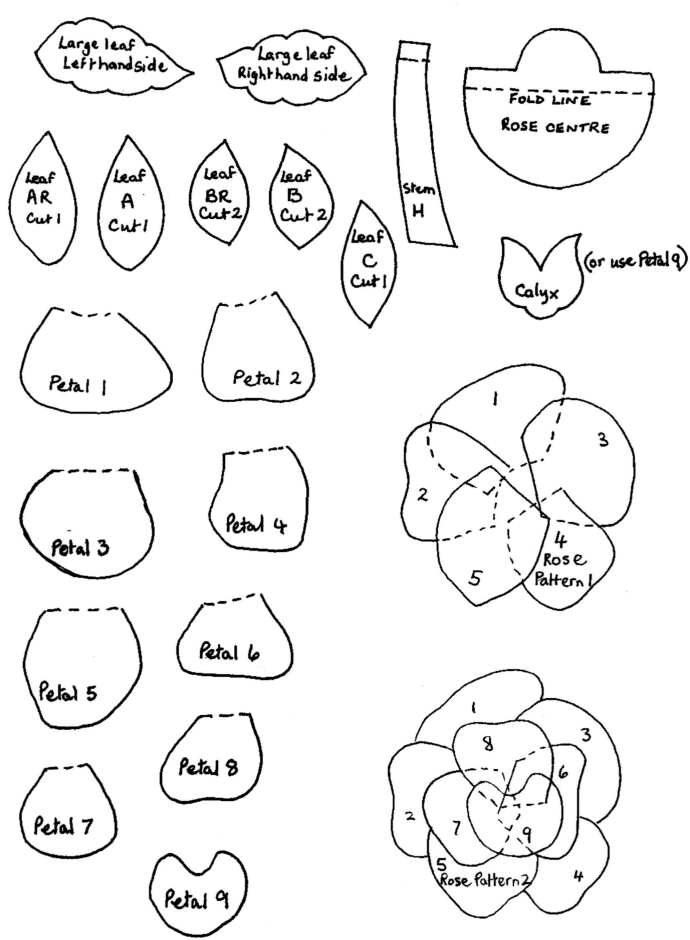

Large leaf Lefthandside

Large leaf Righthand side

Stem H

FOLD LINE
ROSE CENTRE

Leaf AR Cut 1

Leaf A Cut 1

Leaf BR Cut 2

Leaf B Cut 2

Leaf C Cut 1

Calyx (or use Petal 9)

Petal 1

Petal 2

Petal 3

Petal 4

Petal 5

Petal 6

Petal 7

Petal 8

Petal 9

1
3
2
5
4
Rose Pattern 1

1
8
3
6
2
7
9
5
Rose Pattern 2
4

The Quilted Squares

This section describes the creation of the Quilted Squares in the Floral Dimensions Quilt, which alternate with the floral squares.

Requirements

- Thread: machine embroidery thread for candlewicking or small decorative stitch; two different thread colours for machine quilting (colour 1 and colour 2) –these need to show up against the background so either use a 30 weight thread or two 40 weight threads through one needle in either cotton, rayon or polyester
- 4oz polyester wadding: 12in (30.5cm) square approximately
- Water-soluble thread – optional
- Background fabric: 14in (35.5cm) square
- Wadding (batting): 14in (35.5cm) square
- Backing and sashing fabric

Candlewicking

1 Trace the design on to the background fabric using an easily removable marking pen or pencil.

2 Place tear-away stabiliser underneath and sew a candlewicking stitch or small decorative stitch along the dotted lines. Some machines have a French knot or candlewicking stitch built in. If this is not available on your machine you may be able to programme the pattern in. There are two basic ways to do this. Method 1 uses a zigzag stitch so the knot is formed sideways. Method 2 uses the eight-directional feed menu found on some machines, so the stitch will sew forwards and backwards. Try both methods if you can to decide which you prefer. One other suggestion is to repeat a full stop stitch found in the lettering menu but don't cut the straight stitches out between them as they aren't secure enough.

Programme for Method 1:   {zigzag: length 0.0, width 2.0} eight times
straight stitch: length 5.0

Programme for Method 2:   {triple forward stitch, triple backward stitch} four times
triple forward stitch
straight stitch, length 5.0

The top tension may have to be loosened slightly (lower number). Use tear-away stabiliser under your fabric and a foot with a deep groove in the centre of the underside to allow the knots to feed through evenly.

For sewing a candlewicking stitch that follows a curve, use a foot with a wider groove underneath. This gives more room for knots to feed through that are slightly to one side because of the curve. Optional: clip the straight stitch in front and behind each knot after all the candlewicking has been sewn.

To manage sewing the curves, pivot after a complete stitch pattern by counting the number of times the needle goes back and forth or sideways. Alternatively, engage the 'Stop' or 'End of Pattern' button.

3 Remove the stabiliser. Thread your machine with water-soluble thread or a fine weight thread that matches your background, on the top and in the bobbin. Pin a square of 4oz polyester wadding on the wrong side of your background fabric, behind the areas outlined in red on the pattern, placing the pins on the right side. Using a walking foot and a straight stitch, length 3.0, sew along the lines marked in red on the pattern. Turn the square to the wrong side and trim the excess polyester wadding that is outside the stitching lines.

4 Pin the 14in (35.5cm) square of quilt wadding and background fabric to the backing fabric. If you are going to use my 'back-to-front' method to join the squares together you will need to follow the instructions for making up in the Back-to-Front Joining Technique section (Layering the Appliquéd Squares before Quilting), to ensure that the backing is marked correctly at this point. Using a straight stitch, length 3.0 and colour 1 of your selected machine quilting thread, sew around the lines marked in red and in blue on the pattern. If you used a thread to match your background to attach the 4oz wadding, then as you sew remove this thread about an inch at a time in front of the needle. If you used water-soluble thread, spray with water after the square has been quilted and leave flat to air dry.

5 Change to colour 2 and sew around all the lines marked in green on the pattern.

6 Machine quilt the background of the square with your own choice of design, such as echo quilting, stippling, cross hatching or as I did, with parallel lines (described below).

Parallel Line Quilting

These quilting lines are not meant to be exactly the same distance apart or perfectly straight (see photos below) but you will need to draw a few guide lines to prevent them from being too slanted.

1 To mark these guide lines, use an easily removable marker and draw lines approximately 3in (7.6cm) apart, parallel to the sides of the square. These are only meant as a guide and won't necessarily be the actual quilting lines.

2 Begin at the top of the square, about ¼in (6mm) in from the tacking (basting) line on the left. Machine a line parallel to the side to about ¼in (6mm) before the tacking line at the bottom. Leave the needle in the fabric, pivot 90 degrees and sew two stitches along the bottom. Leave the needle in the fabric, pivot again 90 degrees and then sew another almost parallel line to the top of the square.

3 Continue in this way, using the guide lines to keep fairly straight. When you reach a shape that will not be quilted, stop with the needle in the fabric, sew two stitches parallel to the edge of the shape, pivot again and continue filling in all the areas with parallel lines.

Quilted Square – Pattern 1

Additional Notes

Candlewicking: Begin at the top of the flowers at the side of the design and sew to the base. As a guide, place marks on the other side to correspond with the sewn knots. Sew the knots on the other side from top to base.

Quilting Colour 1: On the flowers at the side of the design, sew around the outside, coming into the centre at the division of the leaves. Pivot 360 degrees and sew on the same line, back to the outline again. For the outside of the centre shape, begin at a point and sew to the base of the flower stem. Sew up to the flower, around the outside and back down the stem. Continue to the next point.

Quilting Colour 2: On the corner flowers, begin at a vein on the inner circle. Sew the vein towards the outside, pivot 360 degrees, sew back down the vein towards the centre and along the curve to the next vein. Continue until all veins and the complete circle have been sewn. For the centres of the flowers at the sides, begin at the base and sew the two shapes in a continuous line.

Quilted Square – Pattern 2

Additional Notes

Candlewicking: Begin at the top of the petals that are coming out from the centre and sew to the base. As a guide, place marks on the other side to correspond with the sewn knots. Sew the knots on the other side from top to base. Use the same procedure for the centre and top of the flowers at the corners.

Quilting Colour 1: On the flowers at the corners of the design, begin at the bottom of the stem (on the edge of the centre circle) and sew up to the flower. Sew around the outside of the flower, coming in towards the centre at the division of the leaves. Pivot 360 degrees and sew on the same line, back to the outline. Continue around in this way to the other side of the base of the stem. For the petals coming out from the centre, begin at the base, sew up to the point and then along the curl. Pivot 360 degrees and sew back along the curl and around the diamond. Sew the curl on the other side, back to the point of the petal and down to the base of the petal.

Quilting Colour 2: On the corner flowers, begin at the base on the outside of the oval shape and sew to the first vein in the leaf. Sew to the end of the vein, pivot 360 degrees, sew back down the vein and continue around the oval, sewing all the veins in this way and ending at the base of the oval.

Back-to-Front Joining Technique

This section describes the technique I used to join the quilt blocks,
the corner blocks and the borders.

Layering the Appliquéd Squares before Quilting

1 Cut out a 17in (43.2cm) square of backing/sashing fabric. Place the square, wrong side up, on the imperial grid side of a cutting mat with the edges in line with the grid lines.

2 Using a fabric marker or pencil that won't disappear, draw lines 1½in (3.8cm) in from each edge. This will be your stitching line when joining the squares together.
Use the grid on the mat as your guide, not the fabric edges (see Fig 1).

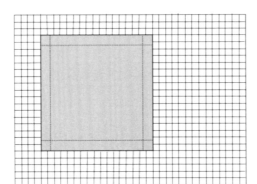

Fig 1

3 Place a 14in (35.5cm) square of wadding in the centre of the backing/sashing fabric. The wadding edges should meet the lines you drew in step 2.

4 Pin the appliquéd square on top of the wadding, lining the edges up as near as possible to the drawn lines. If your background fabric is sewn to the wadding, place the two on top at the same time, omitting the previous step (step 3).

5 Use a disappearing marker or chalk wheel to draw lines on the appliquéd fabric, 2½in (6.3cm) in from the edge of the background/sashing fabric. Again, use the mat as a guide, not the fabric edge. Pin securely.

6 Machine tack (baste) through all the layers along these lines. Be aware though that you will not be quilting beyond these lines.

7 I have used three different quilting patterns on the squares – crosshatching, parallel lines and echo quilting. Decide which one you want to use and then refer to the instructions below to mark and quilt each of the squares.

Quilting the Squares

1 Choose the threads to quilt the squares. Cotton or rayon would be best, although a polyester one could be used. The colour should match closely with the fabric. I used the same 40 weight rayon in the top and in the bobbin. A different shade could be used in the bobbin but check the tension carefully to make sure you don't see any of the bottom thread on the top, or the top thread on the bottom.

2 Use a quilting needle if you have one and a walking foot. Make sure you start with thread tails and adjust your machine to a stitch length 3.0. If your top and bottom threads match then you can 'fix' or 'secure' the stitches at the beginning but leave thread tails. This means lots of ends to pull through and bury but gives a much better result than cutting them off. If the two threads are different shades, using the fix function may result in blobs of the top colour showing on the back. If you choose not to use the fix function, you will have to pull the threads through to the back, knot them and bury the ends. Use an easy-threading needle to save time.

3 When you reach an appliqué shape where the quilting line continues on the other side, fix the stitch (if using), lift the presser foot and using your index finger, pull out the top and bottom thread about 4in (10.2cm) to the side of the machine. When these threads are cut in half, this will leave them long enough to pull through and bury. Move the fabric and position the needle the other side of the appliqué shape at the beginning of the next line and continue as before.

4 Bury the thread tails after sewing a few lines. If you leave them all to the end, they are likely to get sewn in and be really difficult to separate.

5 Optional – quilt around the outside of all flowers and leaves. You may need to use a narrow presser foot or zipper foot in some areas rather than the walking foot.

Crosshatch Quilting

Use an easily removable marker and mark every 1in (2.5cm) along the tacked (basted) lines, beginning and ending at a corner. Join the marks with diagonal lines – see Fig 2. Don't draw the lines past the tacking (basting) stitches and skip over areas that have appliqué shapes – you won't be quilting across these.

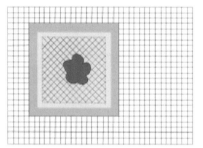

Fig 2

Parallel Line Quilting

These quilting lines are not meant to be exactly the same distance apart or perfectly straight (see photos below) but you will need to draw a few guide lines to prevent them from being too slanted.

1 To mark these, use an easily removable marker and draw lines approximately 3in (7.6cm) apart, parallel to the sides of the square. These are only meant as a guide and won't necessarily be the actual sewing lines.

2 Begin at the top of the square, about ¼in (6mm) in from the tacking (basting) line on the left. Machine a line parallel to the side to about ¼in (6mm) before the tacking line at the bottom. Leave the needle in the fabric, pivot 90 degrees and sew two stitches along the bottom. Leave the needle in the fabric, pivot again 90 degrees and then sew another almost parallel line to the top of the square.

3 Continue in this way, using the guide lines to keep fairly straight. When you reach a shape that will not be quilted, stop with the needle in the fabric, sew two stitches parallel to the edge of the shape, pivot again and continue filling in all the areas with parallel lines.

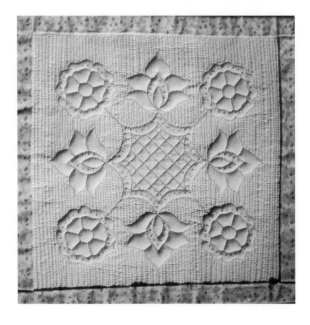

Echo Quilting

Echo quilting is the term used for stitching that echoes the shape of an appliquéd or quilted design, similar to ripples on a pond (see the detail pictures below). The lines are anything from ¼in to ½in (6mm to 1.3cm) apart and can be as many or as few as desired. The colour of the thread will usually match the colour of the fabric you are quilting. You don't always have to use a straight stitch, so experiment with a decorative, wavy, triple, or even a candlewicking or entredeaux stitch.

     The easiest way to echo quilt is to guide the edge of the presser foot or walking foot against the edge of the shape you are echoing for the first line. For the next line, guide the edge of the presser foot against the last sewn line and continue like this. However, if you want to be a little more precise, there are two techniques you can use, as follows.

Method A: At each pivot point, draw a line that bisects the angle. As you sew around the shape, when you pivot on this line you will be the correct distance away from the next edge. This will work at whatever distance you are away from the original shape.

Method B: To be really fussy, you can mark on your pivot lines how far apart you want the lines to be. They are usually the same distance apart, but why not try gradually widening the distance between the lines the farther out you go? Marking them like this will keep everything even, which is important if you are sewing to the edge of a block and want the same number of lines all around your design.

Preparing the Quilted Squares

1 If the quilted squares are distorted, then you may want to 'block' them first. This is done by spraying them lightly with water on both sides and then pinning them to a lace-shaping board or ironing board (Photo 1). If your board doesn't have a grid marked on top, then draw around a 12in (30.5cm) square. Pin the tacked (basted) lines on the square that are on the edge of the quilting to the 12in (30.5cm) square and leave to dry (Photo 2).

Photo 1

Photo 2

2 Trim the wadding and front on the squares a tiny fraction inside the pencil lines wherever they are overlapping the line. Trim the points of the corners of the wadding and front a fraction (see Fig 3).

3 Place one of the squares right side up and pin back the top and wadding around each edge to reveal the pencil lines you marked earlier (Fig 4).

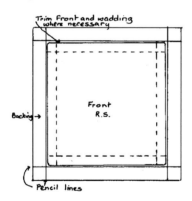

Fig 3

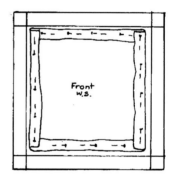

Fig 4

4 Place a quilter's ruler over the pencil line so that the 1in line on the ruler is over the top of one of the pencil lines, and the edge of the ruler is approximately ½in (1.3cm) from the raw edge of the backing (Fig 5). Using a fabric folding pen or hera marker, make a crease on the fabric along the edge of the ruler. Remove the ruler and fold the backing fabric along the crease, wrong sides together. This will give you an approximately ½in (1.3cm) turning and a fold exactly 1in (2.5cm) away from the pencil line. Repeat for the remaining three sides of the square.

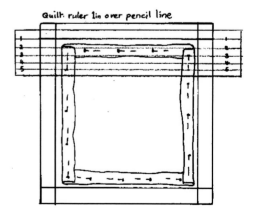

Fig 5

73

5 Remove the pins that are keeping the sides back. Unpick the tacking (basting) stitches at the corners and pin back the wadding and front as in the Photo 3. Place the corner of a quilter's ruler over one of the corners of the square so the pencil lines on the square are under the 1in line markings on the ruler.

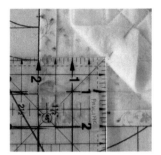

Photo 3

6 Using an air-erasable marker, draw a line on the backing fabric along the edges of the ruler.

7 Remove the ruler and push a pin through the point where the pencil lines cross (Fig 6).

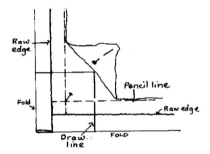

Fig 6

8 Fold the corner of the backing fabric to the opposite corner that was marked with the air-erasable pen, making sure that the diagonal fold you have just made begins and ends at the point where the air-erasable lines meet the edges of the square. The pin should be pointing outwards in the centre of the diagonal folded edge (see Fig 7 and 7A below). Press the edge firmly with an iron.

9 Using a quilter's silver pencil or similar and a ruler, continue the pencil line on both sides to the pin, completing the corner – see Photo 4.

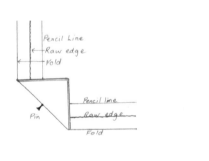

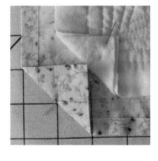

Fig 7   Fig 7A   Photo 4

10 Remove the pin and open out the folded corner. Open out the ½in (1.3cm) turning at the corner and fold it into a blunt mitre – see Figs 8, 9 and 10.

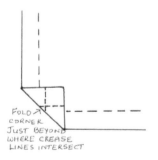

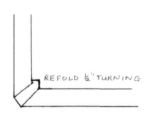

Fig 8   Fig 9   Fig 10

11 Trim back the seam allowances at the ends of the diagonal crease as in Fig 11. See also Photo 5.

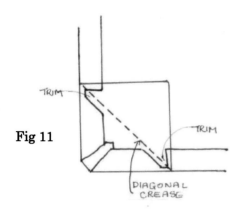

Fig 11

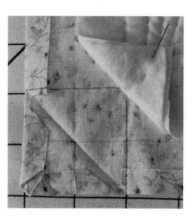

Photo 5

12 Iron a 12in (30.5cm) square of Steam-A-Seam fusible web to the wrong side of the contrasting fabric you have chosen for the corners that are under the cathedral windows on each block and then cut out 112 squares each 1in (2.5cm) square. Peel the backing paper from each square and then iron one square to each corner, a fraction away from the lines, as in Photo 6. Apply a little fabric glue underneath the corner to keep it folded over.

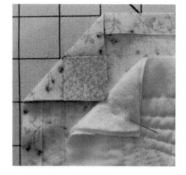

Photo 6

Joining the Squares

1 Arrange all of the squares in their finished order. They will be joined in five rows of five squares.
On the first two squares to be joined, pin back the wadding and background fabric away from the pencil line on the sides that will be joined.

2 Keeping the corners folded along the diagonal crease, pin the two squares together, backs facing, along the pencil line on both squares. Match the corners and pencil lines *exactly*.

3 Sew the seam using a straight stitch, length 2.5, from corner to corner as in Photo 7 below, securing the stitching at both ends. Bury the thread tails. Repeat for the remaining squares of the first row. Press the seams open from both sides – see Photo 8.

Photo 7

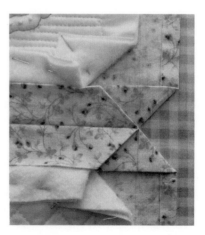

Photo 8

4 Remove the pins holding back the wadding and background and then flatten the fabric underneath the seam allowances and the folded corner.

5 Remove the tacking (basting) that marks the 12in (30.5cm) square. Pin the seam allowance of the backing/sashing fabric down over the background fabric so the edge lies along the line where the machine tacking (basting) was (see Photo 9).

Photo 9

6 Using a buttonhole appliqué stitch, a blind hem stitch or a small zigzag stitch, machine the edge to the square (Photo 10).

Photo 10

7 Using the templates in Fig 12 below, mark the sashing for quilting as shown in Fig 13. Begin and end the design level with where the buttonhole appliqué stitch starts and finishes. Machine quilt along the lines.

Fig 12 (templates actual size)

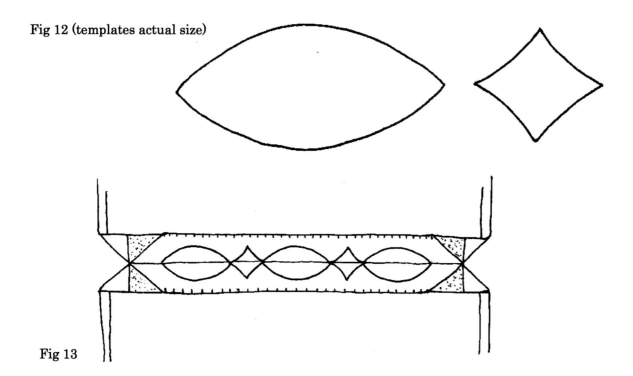

Fig 13

8 Join and quilt the remaining four strips of five squares in the same way.

9 Join the first two strips. First peel back and then pin the wadding and background away from the corner and the line that is to be sewn – see Photo 11. Pin the rows of squares together along the pencil lines, matching the corners *exactly*. Machine along the line (Photo 12).

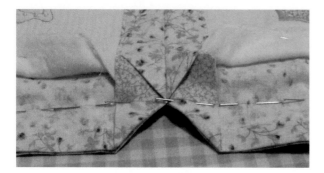

Photo 11

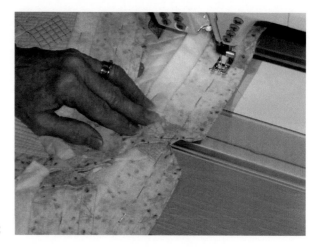

Photo 12

10 Repeat steps 4-7 above to complete joining the squares and quilting the sashing. You may need to trim back the corner of the wadding and background a little before anchoring the sashing to the background so it doesn't bunch up. However, do not cut off too much otherwise the corner will be very weak.

Forming the Mitres

1 To form the mitres, first mark the folded edges of the mitre with an easily removable marker as follows. On both edges, mark a dot ⅛in–¼in (3mm–6mm) from either end, point A, and then mark a dot at point B, midway between the two A points. Next mark a dot at point C, ⅜in (1cm) from point B at either side (Fig 14). Thread a needle with a long length of thread to match the fabric and bring the two ends together so you have two threads hanging from the eye, and then knot the ends together.

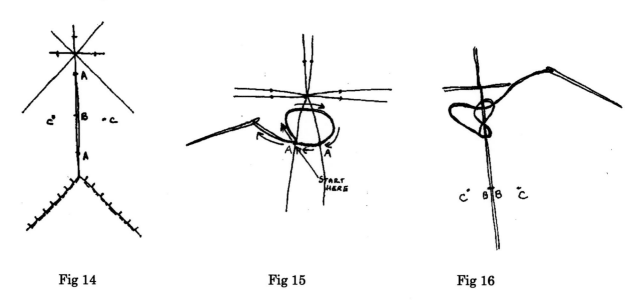

Fig 14   Fig 15   Fig 16

2 Bring the needle up through point A at the centre end of one mitre, on the left side, concealing the knot at the back. Push the needle down on the right side at point A and bring it up again on the left side (Fig 15). Pull the thread so the edges meet. Push the needle down on the right-hand side and up on the left side again. Before pulling the thread tight, twist the loop

77

and pass the needle through the top of the loop (Fig 16). This will form a knot and secure the stitch.

3 Pass the needle through the layers on the left side of the folded edge and bring it out at point B. Bring the edge of point B to point C, securing the stitch as before and forming the turned-back window. Pass the needle through the layers to point A at the other end, secure as before and then repeat for the other side at point B to C (see Fig 17 and also refer back to Fig 14).

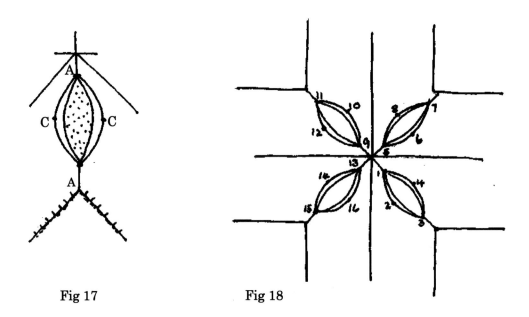

Fig 17   Fig 18

4 Pass the needle between the layers to point A at the centre and then over to the next mitre of the adjoining square. Continue in this way, following the numbered steps in Fig 18 until all four mitres are secured.

5 Repeat this process for all the other mitres on the quilt. This is a little fiddly so if desired, just sew the two folded edges of the mitres together and forget the windows! If you choose not to do the windows then you won't need to add the squares described in Preparing the Squares, step 12.

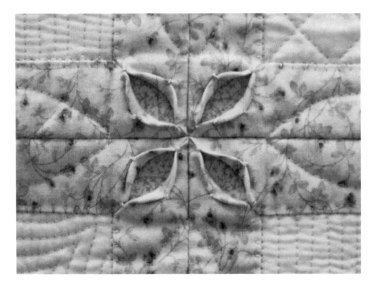

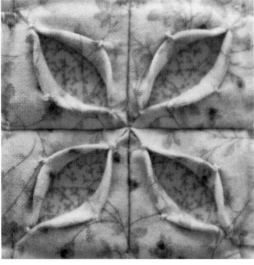

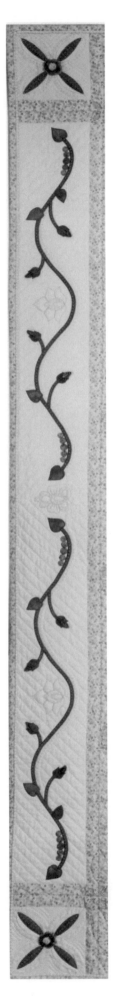

Borders and Corners

This section describes the creation of the borders and the corners on the quilt. The templates are included.

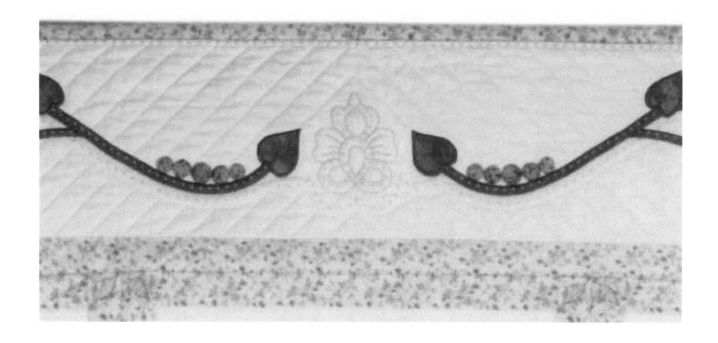

Requirements

- Fabric: for stems, leaves, rosebuds, calyx, circles, corner windows and corner flowers
- Machine sewing thread: cotton or polyester, to match your fabrics
- Machine sewing thread: rayon, cotton or polyester for satin stitching around the leaves
- Background fabric: four strips each 7½in x 73in (19cm x 185.4cm) * and sixteen rectangles each 7in x 4in (17.8cm x 10.2cm)
- Wadding (batting): four strips each 7½in x 73in (19cm x 185.4cm) *, four 7½in (19cm) squares and small amounts for stuffing the leaves
- Backing/sashing fabric: four strips each 9in x 76in (22.9cm x 193cm) * and four 9in (22.9cm) squares
- Contrasting fabric for windows: four 7½in (19cm) squares
- 4oz polyester wadding (batting): 25in (63.5cm) square approximately
- Tear-away stabiliser
- Steam-A-Seam fusible web or Bondaweb
- Wool: for stuffing stems
- Heatproof template plastic or 'Perfect Circles' – optional
- Water-soluble thread – optional

* The sizes given are for using my back-to-front joining technique and twenty-five blocks. Approximately 3in (7.6cm) extra has been added to the length, which will be trimmed before sewing the borders to the quilt. The finished borders are approximately 7½in (19cm) wide.

You will need to join the patterns together to form one half of the border design. For the other half of the design, you will need to trace the pattern on the reverse side to get a mirror image. Use a light box if you have one, or hold the pattern up against a window to see the design through. Crease or mark a line (using an erasable marker) halfway across the length on your background fabric. Use this line to position the pattern for the border design and then trace the design onto the right side of your background fabric.

Stems

1 Cut 1in (2.5cm) wide bias strips and make sixteen rosebud stems each 3½in (8.9cm) long and sixteen rosebud stems each 2¼in (5.7cm) long.

2 Blind hem stitch these stems to the background and then stuff them with wool.

3 Cut 1⅛in (2.8cm) wide bias strips and make eight stems each 19in (48.3cm) long, eight stems 8½in (21.6cm) long and eight stems 8in (20.3cm) long.

4 Blind hem stitch these to the background but do not stuff them yet.

Circles

1 Make thirty-two circles each $^7/_{16}$in (1.1cm) diameter, thirty-two circles each ½in (1.3cm) diameter and sixteen circles each $^9/_{16}$in (1.4cm) diameter.

2 Pin or glue these onto the background and blind hem stitch in place by sewing over the tops of the circles in a row and then underneath them as in Fig 1.

3 Stuff the long stems.

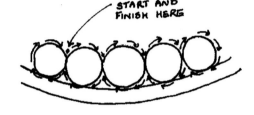

Fig 1

Leaves

1 Trace sixteen of the Large Leaf shape, sixteen of the Medium Leaf, and eight of the Small Leaf on a piece of Steam-A-Seam on the side that has the web attached. Roughly cut them out.

2 Peel off the backing paper that was not drawn on. Press and then iron each leaf on the wrong side of your fabric and cut them out on the lines. Peel off the second backing paper and press the leaves in place on the background.

3 Satin stitch around the edge of the leaves – small leaves width 2.0, medium and large leaves, width 2.5.

4 Place a piece of wadding underneath the background so that it is under a complete leaf. Draw the veins on the leaves with a removable marker. Referring to Fig 2, begin at point A with a triple stitch and sew to point B. Change to a straight stitch and sew to point C, leaving the needle down in the fabric. Turn the fabric around and sew back to point B. Change to a triple stitch and sew to D. Continue in this way, using a triple stitch for the main vein and changing to a straight stitch for the side veins, which will be stitched twice. When you reach point F, change to a straight stitch and outline the leaf all the way around on the inside edge of the satin stitching.

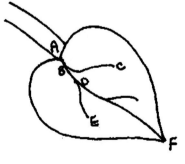

Fig 2

Candlewicking
If desired, sew a candlewicking stitch or similar where indicated by the dots on the pattern.

Rosebuds
Refer to the **Floral Dimensions** book to make thirty-two rosebuds. Sew the base of each bud in place on the background.

Calyx
Refer to the **Floral Dimensions** book (the Rosebud chapter) to make thirty-two calyxes. Place one calyx over each rosebud and blind hem stitch in position.

Trapunto
1 Cut a 4½in (11.4cm) square of 4oz polyester wadding and place this underneath one of the trapunto shapes. Using a water-soluble thread (or a fine thread that will not show) on the top and in the bobbin and a walking foot, sew around the edge of the design, marked in red on the pattern, stitch length 3.0.

2 Turn the background to the wrong side and trim away the wadding that is on the outside of the stitching as close to the stitching as possible.

3 Repeat for the remaining trapunto shapes.

Completing the Borders
1 Draw a line on the wrong side of the backing/sashing border strips, 1½in (3.8cm) from the lower raw edge.

2 Mark the centre of one of the background strips from end to end, either with a pin or a removable marker. Do the same for one of the strips of wadding and one of the strips of backing/sashing fabric.

3 Place the backing/sashing fabric you have just marked, wrong side up on a flat surface. Place the wadding on the top with the top edges even, the bottom edge of the wadding on the line you marked in step 1 and the centre lines matching. Now place the background strip on top, right side up in the same position. You should have 1½in (3.8cm) of backing/sashing fabric extending at the bottom edge and approximately the same extending at either end.

4 Pin and then machine tack (baste) the layers together using a walking foot. Using an easily removable marker, draw a line on the background fabric 1in (2.5cm) up from the raw edge at the bottom and machine tack (baste) along this line. This should be 2½in (6.25cm) from the raw edge of the backing/sashing and where you will quilt up to as you did on the squares.

5 Sew the trapunto shapes in the same way as you did previously in the Quilted Squares chapter.

6 Quilt around the edges of the leaves, stems, circles and buds.

7 Refer to the pattern and quilt a line underneath the candlewicking and the trapunto shapes.

8 Draw a diagonal grid radiating from the centre line and quilt. Do not quilt further than the last leaf at each end and the line you tacked(basted) in step 4 above. Quilt to the top edge where the binding will cover it.

9 Lay your quilt on a flat surface – the floor will do! Place a border strip on top, across the middle, matching the centres of both the quilt and border. Place a mark or pin on the border where the outside edge of the sashing on the last square is. Do the same on the opposite edge.

10 Remove the border and draw a line going through the mark you just made, perpendicular to the top and bottom edges of the border (see Fig 3). Repeat for the other end of the border. This marks the length of your border.

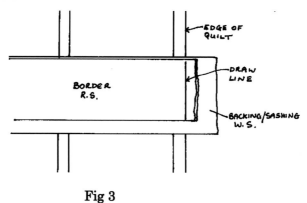

Fig 3

11 Cut the *background and wadding only* along this line, leaving the backing/sashing extending underneath.

12 Now draw a line on the wrong side of the backing/sashing 1½in (3.8cm) from the edge of the wadding and background edge that you just cut. Repeat for the other end of the border strip (Fig 4).

13 Draw a line on the background, 1in (2.5cm) in from the end. Finish sewing the diagonal quilting lines, stopping each one at this line (Fig 5).

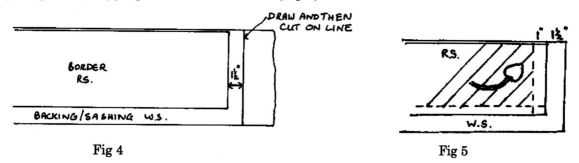

Fig 4   Fig 5

14 Refer to the Back-to-Front Joining Technique section to prepare the sashing along the bottom edge and the ends of the borders before attaching the corners. The top edge will be bound after the borders are attached.

15 Repeat for the remaining border strips.

Corners
1 On the wrong side of each of the four 9in (22.9cm) squares of backing/sashing fabric for the corners, draw a line 1½in (3.8cm) from two adjoining edges.

2 From the background fabric, cut sixteen strips each 7in x 4in (17.8cm x 10.2cm).

3 From the contrasting fabric (that is showing through the windows) and the wadding, cut four 7½in (19cm) squares.

4 Fold each rectangle of background fabric in half, right sides together along the length. Sew a ½in (1.3cm) seam along the top edge – see Fig 6.

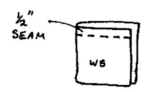

Fig 6

5 Clip the corner and turn the shapes through to the right side. Place the seam in the centre and press it flat.

6 Arrange four of the shapes in a square, with the points in the centre and the seams at the back.

7 Place a ruler over the corner so the raw edges are under the 1in (2.5cm) mark on the ruler – see Photo 1 below. Place a mark on the fabric folded edges where the point of the ruler is.

8 Open out the folded edges of two adjoining quarters and sew them together, right sides facing along the folds, from the raw edge to the mark you made in step 7 – see Photo 2 and Photo 3. Repeat for all the quarters of one corner so they are all sewn together and form a square.

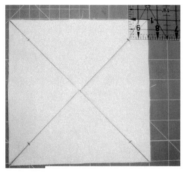
Photo 1

Photo 2

Photo 3

9 Mark ½in (1.3cm) from the point at the centre along each edge. Machine the adjoining edges together with a zigzag stitch, length 2.0, width 1.5, beginning at one mark and sewing across the centre to the opposite mark – see Photo 4.

Photo 4

10 Lightly spray starch the back of the square. Turn the square to the right side and manipulate the window by folding the diagonal folded edges back. Iron in place. Turn the square over and iron it from the back.

11 On the right side of the background fabric, mark approximately ¼in (6mm) from the edge of the window that has been turned back and sew a candlewicking or similar stitch on the line if desired – see Photo 5.

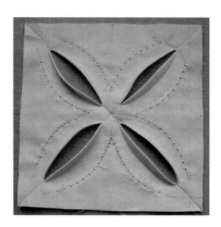

Photo 5

12 Place a 7½in (19cm) square of contrasting fabric underneath the window square, right side up, so the raw edges are even on two of the adjoining sides and ½in (1.3cm) of contrasting fabric extends on the other two sides.

13 Pin a square of 4oz polyester wadding underneath the contrasting fabric. On the right side, peel back the folded edge of each of the window flaps and draw a line along the creases. Using water-soluble thread or fine thread and a walking foot, machine a straight stitch, length 3.0, along the lines to secure the contrasting fabric to the windows and the wadding.

14 Turn the fabric over and trim the wadding that is outside the stitching as close to the stitching as possible – see Photo 6.

Photo 6

15 Place the 9in (22.9cm) square of backing fabric wrong side up and the wadding on top so that two of the adjoining raw edges are even with the backing fabric and the other two adjoining edges are on the lines you drew previously.

16 Place the contrasting fabric with the background fabric sewn to it, right side up on top of the wadding so the edges are even with the wadding (see Photo 7).

Photo 7

17 Machine tack (baste) the layers together ½in (1.3cm) in from the raw edges of the background window fabric.

18 Using a matching thread and walking foot, on the right side, peel back the folded edge of each of the window flaps and machine a straight stitch on top of the stitching you did in step 13, length 3.0, through all thicknesses.

19 Machine echo quilt between the ovals. Sew across the middle over the zigzag stitching in both directions. This will secure the centre and be covered by the flower.

20 Hand sew the window flaps to the background in the middle of the edge of the flap.

21 If the fabric is very thick along the edges that are to be bound, you can trim away ½in (1.3cm) of the second layer and the one underneath that.

22 Repeat for the other three corners.

23 Refer to the **Floral Dimensions** book to make a begonia flower for the centre of each of the four corners but use the 'Centre Flower Petal' template from the border pattern for the petals. Hand sew the flowers in place.

24 Refer to the Back-to-Front Technique section to prepare the sashing on the two sides of each corner. The other two sides will be bound later. Sew one corner to both ends of two of the borders. The top edge will be bound after the borders are attached.

25 Sew the two borders without the corners to two opposite sides of the quilt and then sew the two remaining borders to the other two sides. Refer to the Back-to-Front Technique section to mitre the corners.

Corner and Border Templates

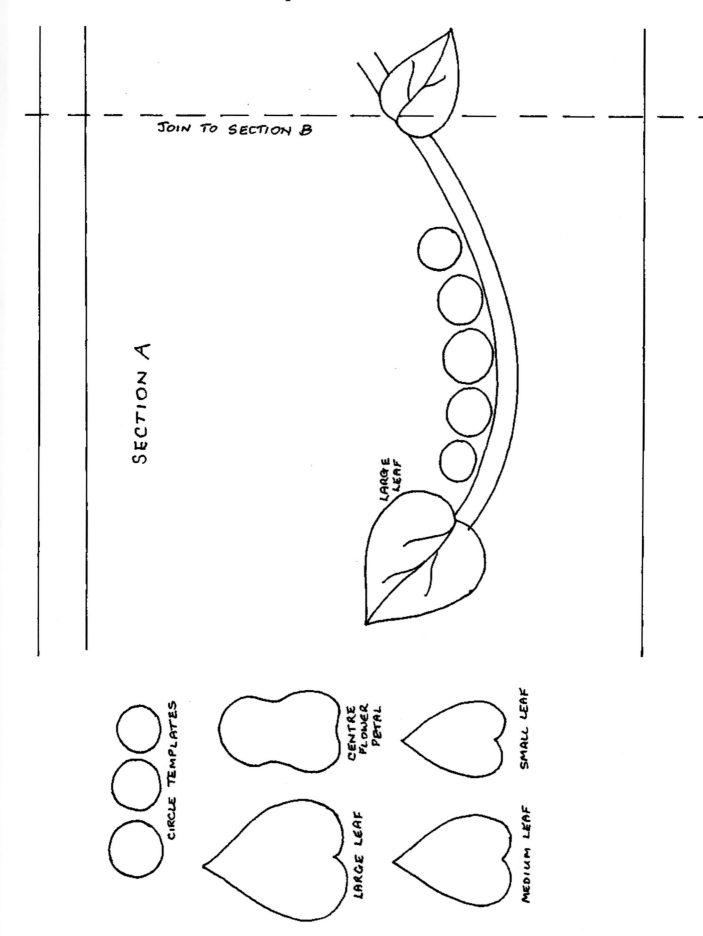

JOIN TO SECTION B

SECTION A

LARGE LEAF

CIRCLE TEMPLATES

CENTRE FLOWER PETAL

SMALL LEAF

LARGE LEAF

MEDIUM LEAF

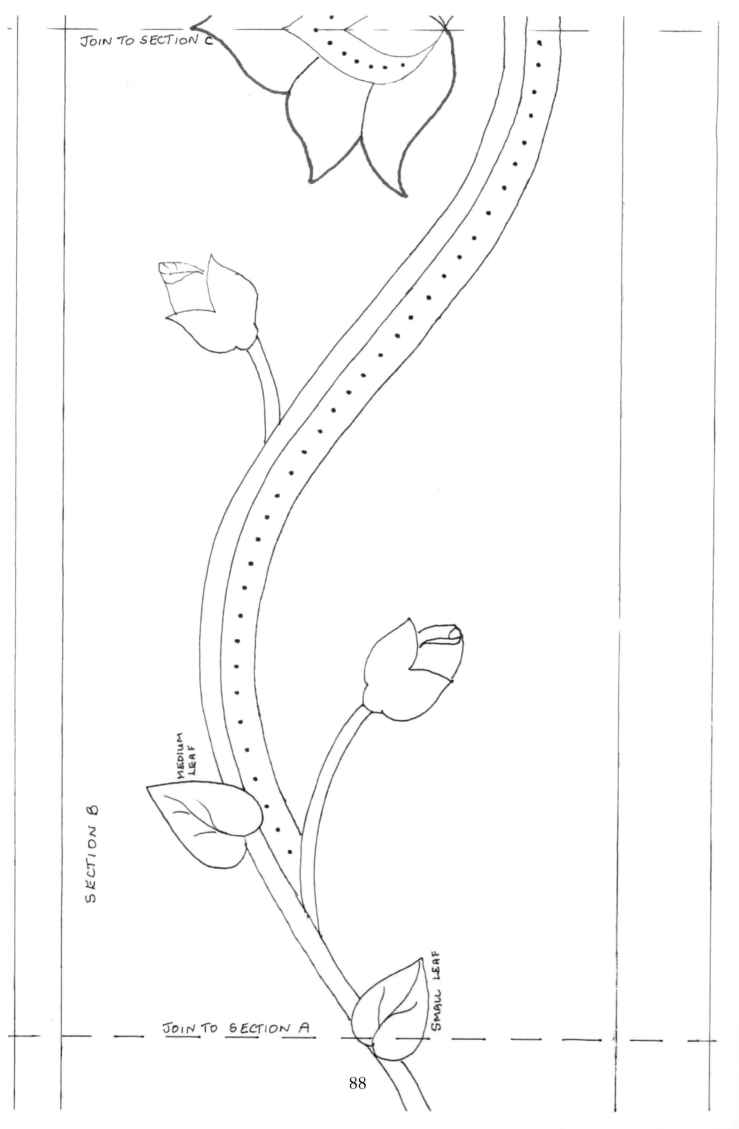

JOIN TO SECTION C

JOIN TO SECTION A

SECTION B

MEDIUM LEAF

SMALL LEAF

88

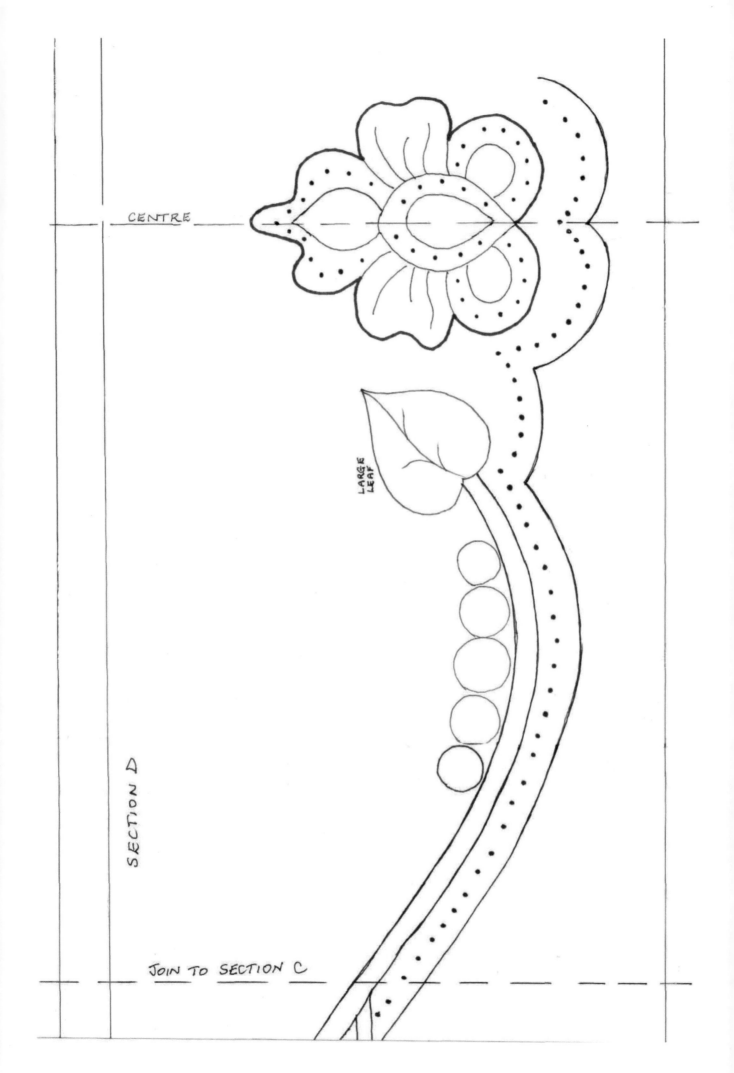

CENTRE

LARGE LEAF

SECTION D

JOIN TO SECTION C

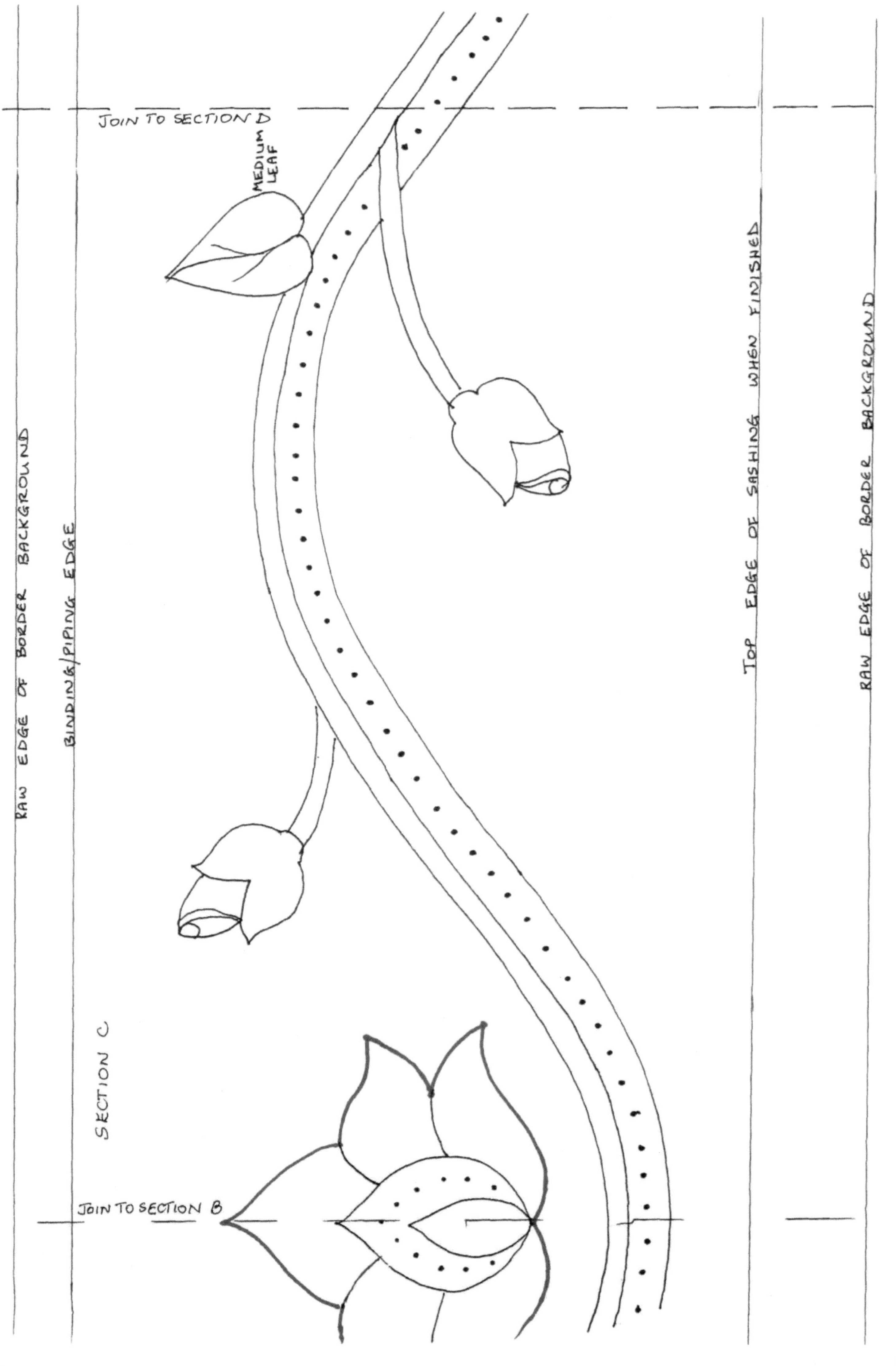

RAW EDGE OF BORDER BACKGROUND

BINDING/PIPING EDGE

JOIN TO SECTION D

MEDIUM LEAF

TOP EDGE OF SASHING WHEN FINISHED

RAW EDGE OF BORDER BACKGROUND

SECTION C

JOIN TO SECTION B

Finishing Off

This section describes adding piping to the quilt between the border and the binding, and also binding the edge of the quilt.

Piping

Adding piping to a project gives a very elegant and professional finish. I like to insert it between the border and the binding on a quilt. You can, as I did, sew a decorative stitch on the fabric before wrapping it around the cord. If you choose to do this, you will need to sew the stitching about $^1/_{16}$in (1.5mm) to one side of the centre of the strip – see Fig 1 below. This will mean that the stitches will sit slightly on the top of the piping rather than on the edge.

You don't need to cut the fabric that covers the cord on the bias unless you are piping a curved edge. If you need to join the strips, do so with a diagonal seam – see step 2 of the technique Double-Fold Binding with Mitred Corners, described below. The width of your fabric strips needs to be twice the width of the seam allowance plus enough to go all the way around the cord. I use $^3/_{16}$in (4mm) wide cord and cut the strips 1⅝in (4.1cm) wide.

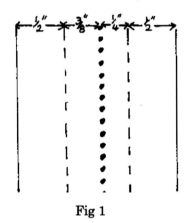

Fig 1

1 Cut the strips of fabric to cover the piping and finger press the fabric piping strip in half, wrong sides together. Open the fabric out flat again and sew a decorative stitch down the length if desired – see Fig 1 above.

2 Wrap the fabric strip around the cord so that the cord sits in the fold. Use either a piping foot or zipper foot and move the needle over slightly to the right, away from the piping, so that the stitching line will not be right next to the piping. This will prevent this line of stitching from showing when the piping has been inserted. Lengthen your stitch to 3.5 and sew to the end of the strip.

3 Trim the piped strip to ½in (1.3cm), or to your required seam allowance from the edge of the piping cord.

4 Align the raw edges of the piped strip with the raw edges of the top edge of the quilt/project. If you have decorated the piping strip, make sure you place the piping up the right way so that the stitching is slightly on the top rather than underneath. Keeping the needle in the same position and the stitch length at 3.5, sew the piping to the edge.

5 Cut the piped strip off in line with the ends of the quilt. Continue in this way, sewing the piped strip to the quilt top on all four sides.

6 Pin the binding (or fabric that will go the other side of the piping) to the edge of the quilt, right sides together. Position the needle so you will be sewing right next to the edge of the piping cord that is sandwiched between the layers, and machine through all the layers with a 3.0 stitch length (see Fig 2 below). The first two rows of stitching should not be showing as they will be in the seam allowance.

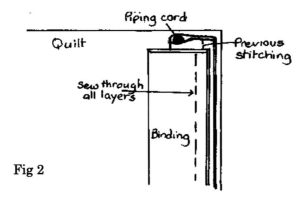

Fig 2

Double-Fold Binding with Mitred Corners

A double-fold binding gives a more durable edging to a quilt than single-fold binding and will stand the test of time.

1 Before beginning the binding, tack (baste) the edges of the quilt ¼in (6mm) from the edge all round using a walking foot.

2 Cut the binding across the grain, i.e., in the opposite direction to the straight grain. There is no need to cut a quilt binding on the bias unless it is to go around a curved edge. There is, however, a little 'give' in the fabric along this grain so the binding won't look too taut. The cut binding width should be six times the finished binding width plus ¼in (6mm). For ½in (1.3cm) finished binding, cut the width to 3¼in (8.2cm). The length of the binding should be the perimeter of the quilt plus about 10in (25.4cm). Join the strips with diagonal seams (see Fig 3).

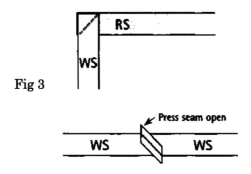

Fig 3

3 Fold and press the binding in half along the length, with wrong sides together. Leave about 8in (20cm) of binding loose at the beginning and start about 8in (20cm) before a corner. With right sides together, align the cut edges of the binding with the cut edges of your quilt. Using a walking foot, sew a shy ½in (1.3cm) seam allowance or a seam allowance just shy of the finished width of your binding. At the corner, stop sewing the width of the seam allowance away from the corner with the needle down in the fabric (Fig 4A). Lift the presser foot and sew off diagonally to the corner. Cut the threads and remove your work from the machine. Fold the binding diagonally up at a 45 degree angle and in line with the next edge of the quilt (Fig 4B).

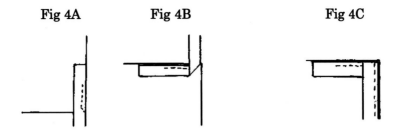

Fig 4A   Fig 4B   Fig 4C

4 Fold the binding down parallel to the next side of the quilt with the raw edges matching and the fold at the top even with the first edge (Fig 4C). Begin sewing at the folded binding at the top and continue sewing to the next corner. Continue in this way, mitring all the corners until you are about 10in (25.4cm) from where you started. Remove the quilt from the machine to join the binding ends together.

5 You should have an 8in (20cm) tail of binding where you started and another tail left at the end with a 10in (25.4cm) gap between the two ends where the binding is not sewn to the quilt. Open out the end of the binding and lay this width across the edge of the quilt in the middle of the unbound length (Fig 5). Mark the quilt with pins or chalk at the edges of the opened binding.

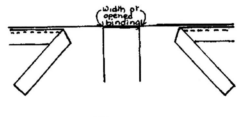

Fig 5

6 Cut the binding on the right where the left-hand mark is (Fig 6A) and the binding on the left where the right-hand mark is (Fig 6B).

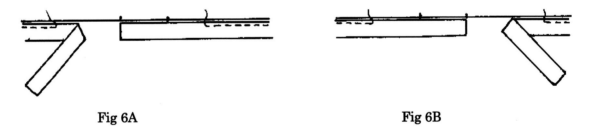

Fig 6A   Fig 6B

7 Place the two ends of binding right sides together and turn the binding that is on the top 90 degrees. Join the two ends with a diagonal seam (Fig 7A). Trim the seam allowance to ¼in (6mm), press the seam open and re-fold the binding wrong sides together.

Fig 7A

8 Put the work back on the sewing machine and finish binding with the joined binding (Fig 7B).

Fig 7B

9 Fold the binding to the back. The front should form neat mitres at the corners. On the back, tuck the fullness at the corners to the opposite side that the front fullness is on. Slipstitch the binding edge, just beyond the stitching line, all around the quilt.

A Final Note...

Now that your Floral Dimensions Quilt is finished you can admire your flowers without the thought of having to weed them, water them or deal with black spot! One final task remains and that is to create a label for the back of your quilt so all its admirers down the years will know some of the details of its creation and marvel at the skill that went into its making. Details you might include are: your name, the date the quilt was created, who it was made for or for what special occasion it was made. You could simply use a permanent fabric marker pen to write the details on a piece of fabric and appliqué it on to the back of the quilt, or hand stitch the details in backstitch. If you own a sophisticated sewing machine you could stitch a more ornate label using machine text, perhaps adding a decorative border.